Kicked int<

the life and ·
Thomas Cook's ama
1910 – 1966

This book is dedicated to all players, officials and club supporters past and present of the 'house' XV's that contributed to the amateur game; who fostered social friendships, in the finest tradition of Thomas Cook, playing for fun in what is the best team game in the world.

John Dann

Front cover images:
(inset) Thos. Cook & Son's RFC First XV
Ravensbourne Club House, 1961/2 season
(main) action against RC Hilversum 1961

Back cover image:
Scrumaging at the home ground Ravensbourne, Kent

All images copyright the author except where acknowledged

The right of John Dann to be identified as the author
of this work has been asserted by him in accordance with
section 77 of the Copyright, Designs and Patents Act, 1988

A CIP catalogue record for this book
is available from the British Library.

ISBN 978-1-84426-931-0

Every effort has been taken to contact copyright owners.
I apologise in advance for any omissions
and would be pleased to insert the appropriate
acknowledgement in any subsequent edition.

Typeface: Bookman Old Style

Printed: printondemand-worldwide.com
Peterborough PE2 6XD

Published by Fastprint
2010

Contents

Page

Acknowledgements--------------------- 4

1 Introduction---------------------------- 5

2 The Thinking Man's Game------------ 7

3 Company world of Cooks------------- 19

4 Cook players – part one & two------- 31

5 Cook players – part three------------- 43

6 The Opponents------------------------- 63

7 Hilversum Easter Tours--------------- 97

8 Club Social Life------------------------ 121

9 Final no side--------------------------- 149

10 Fifty-seven old farts & other quotes- 153

Reference sources --------------------- 155

Appendix:
1. known players 1953-1965--------- 157
2. Some fixture lists 1953-1965----- 161
3. Frequent opponents 1953-1965-- 174

Author---------------------------------- 177

Acknowledgements

Tracing ex players has been difficult –many had left the company and contacts were lost. However, I would like to thank the following for help in making this short story possible. Stewart Grant, Thomas Cook Group Pensions Manager, whose positive encouragement helped establish contact with some past players. Katie Glindon helped as did Jenie Lawrence with the promotion at the annual 'Family Gathering' day. Avril Lavender, past Editor, Thomas Cook Pensioner's Association *'Bulletin'*, kindly gave this project front page treatment, and succeeding Editor Ruth Breckman offered the book publicity. A special thanks to company archivist at Thomas Cook Paul Smith, who helpfully sourced related company material, which is reprinted with their kind permission. His initial research on the sports club pointed me in the right direction with useful articles and photographs featured in various staff publications. This saved many hours (possibly days in my case) of rummaging.

Ex players; Roy Butcher found time to accompany me exploring the Thomas Cook archives whilst also adding some of his own memories, and Roy Bannister who responded to my plea taking much time with emails and telephone conversations to fill vital gaps in my research, and whose dry wit and stories has helped the writing. Mike Lakin supplied a team photo to promote the idea and provided many anecdotes. Pete Simmonds reminded me of past players and Robin Garrett, responded with memories of club characters, and provided a 'missing' 1963/4 fixture list. Harry Masterton-Smith who I traced to Somerset, whose memory I plundered for many après game anecdotes which has provided flavour to the story. Club Captain Hugh Dalzell who I discovered in Devon provided many useful memories, additional photos and club memorabilia, and Mike Lidbetter who also added his memories.

Piet van den Deijssel and Wim van Spengen, Rugby Club Hilversum, who helped with research, Michael Whitfield, Chairman, Barnes RFC, who updated me on the old Harrodian club, Anna Stone, Group Archivist, Aviva, who helped with information on Commercial Union's Cuaco club, Michael Rowe and Helen Burbage, RFU World Rugby Museum, Twickenham, who researched club affiliations, Morgannis Graham, Prudential Group archivist, who explained about the Ibis club, Jamie Boon, Holbrook RFC who responded with details of their predecessor club, the Sun Alliance. The club historians at: Barbarians, Battersea Ironsides, Beccehamians, Beckenham, Brighton Blues, British Airways, Enfield-Ignations, GWR, HAC, Kings College Hospital, London French, London Irish, London New Zealand, London Scottish, Old Caterhamians, Rosslyn Park, RUMS, Saracens, Sidcup and Wasps.

An extract from *Talking of Rugby*, An Autobiography by Bill McLaren published by Hutchinson, is reprinted by kind permission of the Random House Group Ltd.

1. Introduction

The idea for writing this club history has been fermenting for far too long and sadly in the meantime many old players have left the field of play for the last time, taking their stories with them. This is a something of a memoir as well as a story about a group of Thomas Cook players, the world and times we lived in, and the opponents we played. And yes a total nostalgia for the fun we enjoyed particularly the *'drinkfests'* as one club player Harry Masterton Smith called them, combined with a passion for the amateur game that brought us all together. Thos. Cook & Son's Rugby Football Club no longer exists. The rugby section was founded in 1910 -part of a wider company Sports Club formed in the late 19th century. It was originally known as the *'Ludgate Circus Club XV'* –with a name change in 1926 to *Thos. Cook & Son's RFC* after moving to a new head office in Berkeley Street. Despite the interruptions of two world wars it continued until 1966 until eventually –like old soldiers, just faded away. The country had progressed from post-war rationing, to the travel boom in the 1950's and into the social and political changes of the swinging sixties. The firm remained as resilient as ever, and despite increasing competition, it still remained the largest travel agency. The First and 'A' XV 'house' teams, played against many different clubs (far more than would ever be possible today) including some creditable games against some of the old established clubs like *London Irish, Wasps* and *Saracens.*

I had learnt my rugby as a schoolboy in Wales, where it was and remains something of a religion. I can still hear the repeated touch line wailing of the rugby master, his lilting Welsh voice drifting over the Pontcanna playing fields alongside the river Taff (occasionally before a game we'd have to chase the sheep off the pitch, yes really),' *lo-oo-ow, take them low',* and *'scythe them down like corn boys, scythe them down'*, referring to his instilled method of tackling below the waist. Anything above was considered effete. After leaving school I was joining the Merchant Navy to 'see the world'. However, I had found myself in Berkeley Street in the summer of 1959 where I was invited to join Thos. Cook & Sons instead, as the company was then known. I was appointed a junior clerk at four pounds per week and sent to their office located in the *Army & Navy* store (how ironic) in Victoria Street. I had been nursing some grand thoughts of joining the *London Welsh*, a club which was the focus of many exiled Welshmen in London. The club officials at the Old Deer Park however had different ideas. They took their rugby very seriously because playing for them at the time was a number of talented individuals like JPR Williams who would become legends. At sixteen I wasn't very serious, I just wanted to enjoy my rugby and have fun. So I took the social option, and contacted the rugby section of the company's sports club. After a trial I was invited to join the 'A' XV team under the Captaincy of Don Keston for the 1959-60 Season. It was to be my first season in 'club' rugby. It was my right of passage – I also drank beer, learnt a few songs and met girls. I continued to enjoy playing for five seasons until an inconvenient motor cycle accident cut short my playing career. I remained with Cook's a few more years, working in the Publicity Department under the irascible eye of Bill Cormack selling advertising space to the likes of Peter Hofmann of the *Hotel Du Lac* in Interlaken, persuading them to part with their money. This 'house' club history is a light-hearted look at the people and times we played in. It is based on material from the company archives, personal memorabilia and old photographs. It also contains the memories of some surviving ex players. One of whom, Roy Bannister, commented *'sometimes I can't remember what I've climbed the stairs for – let alone forty years ago'*. So this is the result, any inaccuracies are mine and Anno Domini alone.

John Dann
Hove, East Sussex, 2010

2. The Thinking Man's Game

"Through sport, boys acquire virtues which no books can give them, not merely daring and endurance, but, better still, temper, self-restraint, fairness, honour, unenvious approbation of another's success, and all that "give and take" of life which stands a man in good stead when he goes forth into the world, and without which, indeed, his success is always maimed and partial".

Charles Kingsley (1815-1875)
Writer of children's stories and Chaplain to Queen Victoria

To understand rugby and the passion it stirs, it would help to know a little of its history. This is an eclectic story of how rugby came into being, and how it evolved over the years. It's also about some of its players, who were innovative, brave, eccentric and helped establish a game, which is much more than just a mere winter pastime for muddied oafs, as Kipling described. This just might allow the reader to gain insight into why boys and even old boys play up, and play the game.

As Jean-Pierre Rives one time French rugby captain declared, *'The whole point of rugby is that it is, first and foremost, a state of mind, a spirit.'* Jeremy Guscott, the ex England International, whose surprise drop goal in the dying minutes clinched a victory for the 1997 British Lions' in South Africa, continued the theme by saying *'Deep down, most good rugby players are free-spirited'*. There is this thread of non-conformism and spirit running through the history of the game and the players who played it. Legend has it that a boy called William Webb Ellis picked up the ball during a football match at Rugby School in 1823, which probably confused his friends at the time. In those days Football meant just that – using your feet to kick the ball. In the mayhem that followed, the boys of Rugby School realised how much fun they could have with the game that Webb Ellis had unexpectedly created. It was a thrill to run with the ball, (these were made by local boot and shoe maker William Gilbert, whose name still appears on rugby balls today) to test one's strength against others' and to meet a more physical challenge.

There is a commemorative plaque on the Headmaster's Wall in the Close at Rugby School, known as the Webb Ellis stone, describing the boy's sudden wild enthusiasm rather appropriately. Part of the inscription reads '... *who with a fine disregard for the rules of football as played in his time first took up the ball in his arms and ran with it, thus originating the distinctive feature of the rugby game...*'. The first rules, (because they were called that then), were drawn up over three days in the summer of 1845 by three senior boys of Rugby school one of which was the seventeen year old son of the headmaster, Dr Arnold, after they had been asked to codify the game.

The game of course kept a large number of boys safely occupied in a restricted space for hours at a time. In the beginning, up to a hundred boys could play in a single match, as reported in *Tom Brown's Schooldays'*, a novel written by another Rugby School pupil Thomas Hughes, in 1857 (describing the actions between the 'dodgers' and the 'chargers'). In the early days games were settled by kicking goals, the best out of three. The team was allowed to 'try' to kick a goal if it touched the ball down in the area behind the other team's goal, which is why it was called a 'try'. Rugby was the game, and what had once been little more than a free-for-all between two sides, a riotous assembly, where a boy could make a name for himself by his pluck, gradually became the testing ground of character. Defeat would teach pride, and victory humility. Boys would learn courage in pursuit of glory, teamwork in adversity, and a stoical reaction to physical pain. The ultimate test of character was to stand up and be counted, not to flinch, to run the ball hard and straight at the opposition and then to stand and tackle, when in their turn as they were bound to do they fiercely ran it back. 'Muscular Christianity' – as it became known, was quickly adopted by the new Victorian public schools.

In January 1871 the Rugby Football Union was founded in the *Pall Mall* restaurant in Regent Street London (restaurants and pubs feature frequently in rugby club formations) to bring some sort of order, and standardise, the many variations of rules in the game. For example clubs in Scotland played twenty-a-side; as well removing some of the more violent aspects of the Rugby School game. A committee was formed by three ex-Rugby School pupils, who by this time were all lawyers, and were invited to help formulate a set of rules. Being lawyers they formulated '*laws*' not '*rules*'. This task was completed and approved by June 1871.

Then in August 1895 a meeting at the George hotel in Huddersfield (the home town of an old Thomas Cook player), irreversibly changed the face of rugby. A number of Northern Clubs created the Northern Rugby Union –eventually to become Rugby League in 1922. The southern-based RU had charged several of these clubs with professionalism. They argued it was about 'broken time' payments for players that lost wages, either while playing or recovering from injuries sustained on the field of play. This broke the amateur code, and unable to agree, the professional League and the amateur Union game split. It took another hundred years for this to change.

Around much the same time, a French educator and rugby enthusiast, Baron Pierre de Coubertin (1863-1937), was instrumental in bringing the first English club, *Rosslyn Park* to Paris, in 1892, playing a match against *Stade Francais*. The same year de Coubertin made the first public call to revive the Olympic Games and the first modern Olympics were held in Athens in 1896. However, de Coubertin's original sporting love was rugby. Intrigued by what he had read about English public schools, particularly Thomas Arnold, Headmaster of Rugby, who he describes as '*the leader and classic model of English educators,*' he visited England to see for himself. What he saw on the English playing fields, he later wrote in a book, '*organised sport can create moral and social strength*'. Not only did organised games help to set the mind and body in equilibrium, it also prevented the time being wasted in other ways. First developed by the ancient Greeks, it was an approach to education that he felt the rest of the world had forgotten and to whose revival he was to dedicate the rest of his life. On returning he became one of the founders of the game in France, and set up the first French schools championship in 1890. He was the first writer to describe rugby as a *'first-rate educational tool'*. In an essay six years later he wrote, *'What is admirable in (rugby) football is the perpetual mix of individualism and discipline, the necessity for each man to think, anticipate, take a decision and at the same time subordinate one's reasoning, thoughts and decisions to those of the captain.'*

At home some innovative players introduced changes to the union game as it developed, which became adopted worldwide. In 1884, Frank Hancock, one of the younger directors of the powerful Welsh brewing family, William Hancock & Co., joined the *Cardiff* first team as a centre three-quarter back. He soon became involved in one of the great tactical innovations of the era. It had been customary to play just three men in the three-quarter line, two wings and a centre. Hancock decided to experiment with four, inserting an extra centre. Using this system Cardiff had an invincible record in 1885/6 as a result of their greater flexibility in attack. Wales then adopted the two-centre formation and after a few difficult seasons this new formation was accepted throughout the rugby playing world. (By coincidence many years later, I was born in his old family home *Gwaunfarren House* in Merthyr Tydfil, by then it had been requisitioned as a nursing home during World War Two). Other changes were introduced by Wavell Wakefield (*Harlequins*), a man very much ahead of his time, who once commented *'It is because the freedom of rugger and its consequent risks that it breeds hardiness, which in these days of cocktails and lounge lizards is a quality to be encouraged.'* His innovations helped to bring England great success in the 1920's. He shaped forward play as we know it today. Baron Wakefield of Kendal as he later became known (*Wakers'* to his team-mates), saw the weakness of the haphazard way scrums were formed by throwing groups of forwards together in whatever order they arrived on the scene. Wakefield decided that specialist positions for the forwards would improve the game. He increased forward mobility to develop the art of loose play. Fly-halves have Wakefield to thank for the painful tradition of being flattened by a speedy open-side flanker if they take to long over a decision.

The game's Victorian values were to be tested fully on the outbreak of World War One. In war rugby's ruling-classes had found the ultimate expression for the values they held so dear, an ethos of individual strength and teamwork born on the playing fields of early Victorian public schools. Rugby players made good soldiers, and equally soldiers made good rugby players. The Rugby Football Union sent out a circular urging all its players to enlist. Entire rugby clubs had joined up en masse, and Rugger could soon boast its very own war heroes. Like Edgar Mobbs of *Northampton & England,* he was over age but raising his own sportsman company, used to lead his men 'over the top' by punting a rugger ball into no-man's land ahead of the attack. And the flaxen-haired Ronnie Poulton-Palmer (*Rugby School & Harlequins*), of Huntley & Palmer biscuits, who ran in four breathtaking, tries from centre on his last international appearance for England in 1914. He joined the *4th Berkshires* and was shot dead by a sniper in Belgium in 1915. Mobbs was killed in 1917 at Ypres. Every year since 1921 in March the *Barbarians* play a team from the East Midlands in the annual Edgar Mobbs Memorial Game. There is now a Memorial Ground in Bristol dedicated '*to those who played in the Great Game during the season 1914 -1918*'.

Britain has a long tradition of welcoming people to these shores (and resourceful rugby administrators often find a way to bend the nationality rules when a player is good enough). One such player was a Russian Aristocrat. His parents had fled to England after the

Russian Revolution in 1917. The young Prince Alexander Obolensky played for *Oxford University* and later *Rosslyn Park* and had shown himself to be an elegant winger with speed. Selected for England he became a legend with his two famous tries against the *All Blacks* in 1936 in front of the Prince of Wales at Twickenham. He was introduced to Obolensky before the match and was heard to observe *'I thought I was the only prince here today'*. The match was all captured on newsreel. At 13-0 this was England's first victory over New Zealand and there was only one hero *'Obo'*. He later joined the RAF, in his adopted country at the outbreak of World War Two, and was killed in a landing accident in his Hurricane fighter in 1940. Today, Twickenham honours his memory with the *Obolensky Suite* a glass-fronted hospitality room overlooking the pitch in the East Stand. The inter-war years saw more rugby clubs founded in England than in any other decade, with many schools changing from Association football. The growth of the rugby playing grammar and public schools eventually produced many old boy sides which formed a strong part of Thos. Cook & Son's fixture list. It was the common perception in the south east of England, (not completely true) that Old Boy sides were really a bunch of marauding, beer-swilling, guffawing circle of 'Hurray Henry's', well-stuffed with solicitors, surveyors, bankers and the like. In their world, with the ending of schooling, boys never became men, but just older boys. We visited their clubhouses and enjoyed their hospitality. I learnt many rugby songs with their simple lyrics, and repetitive verses, the melodies, some of which still linger to this day. They were a bastion of what would be often called 'rugger-buggers', – players who are keenly interested in the game and actively partake in the ethos of the sport, noted for its boisterous social behaviour and macho image.

The game's Victorian values were still being advocated as late as 1944, when the author E D H Sewell, published *Rugger: The Man's Game*, in which he proposed a post-war Ministry of Sport and compulsory Rugger. (*'Quite right sir'!)*

Rugby has the distinction of bringing people together in a way no other field game does, (consider the scrum), but is particularly demonstrated with overseas tours of the *British Lions'* and domestic tours of the *Barbarians.* The four home nations (and uniquely in rugby, Ireland is one country) came together in 1910 with the first ever overseas tour to South Africa. To play for the *British Lions'* remains the ultimate accolade for any home union rugby player. But it wasn't until 1971 that the Lions won a series for the very first time. Three years later, under the Captaincy of the legendary Irishman Willie John McBride they completed a tour of South Africa unbeaten. Playing Test rugby in South Africa is brutal, and had never been won by a Lions side, that is until a certain W.J.McBride's XV arrived. Willie John McBride the Ulsterman will forever be associated with a special number –'ninety-nine'. It is the number that symbolised the refusal of the 1974 British Lions' to be bullied and beaten into submission by the Springboks, a process the Lions felt their host referees had allowed for too long on tour. 'Ninety-nine' was the call during the third test in Port Elizabeth, when McBride's players heard it they knew it was the order to attack their closest South-African-Test opponent. It was dirty and outrageous, and it worked. As he said later *'I believe there is a great secret in life. It is realising when to work, and when to play. Those 1974 Lions knew it and that was most important....I knew I could rely on them when I needed them to be at their best.'* The Lions won their first series in South Africa 3-0 with one test drawn. They arrived at Heathrow to cheering crowds.

The *Barbarians* club was formed much earlier by Percy (Tottie) Carpmael, who had been part of an invitation team enjoying a tour of the North. After a late and agreeable dinner in Bradford in 1890 decided that these end of season jaunts should become regular fixtures and so the *Barbarians* were born. Inspired by his personal playing experiences with both *Blackheath* and *Cambridge University*, his dream was to spread good fellowship amongst all rugby football players. They have no ground, clubhouse or subscription and membership was by invitation only. All things great about the open game, flair, courage, spirit and passion - are encapsulated in one great team, called the *Barbarians*. They wear a distinctive black and white hooped jersey, but players retain their individual club socks. (A style adopted by *Thos. Cook's* 'A' team). After a tour of the UK, an overseas team's last match against the *Barbarians* or Baa-Baa's as they were nicknamed, whilst keenly fought, is traditionally a joyous occasion, a festival of running rugby for both sides.

The idea of numbering players shirts didn't really seem to matter to the various rugby unions, as there were no hard and fast rules governing the names of the positions or the numbers worn. It was gradually introduced in the 1920's and used for the first time in the international between Wales and England in 1922. Later when Scotland played England in the Calcutta cup at Twickenham in 1928 King George V asked a former president of the Scottish Football Union James Aikman Smith why Scotland were not wearing numbers and was told *'This sir is a rugby match not a cattle sale'*. By the 1950's all five nations were using numbering systems from 1 to 15 although Ireland and France did this in the reverse order to everyone else. To add to the confusion some clubs omitted the number 13, (like Bath and Richmond) whilst other used letters like Bristol and Leicester. Luckily for the spectator since 1967 it has all been agreed by the International Rugby Board -IRB (founded 1886) who administer the laws and regulations, that jersey numbering is standardised worldwide. (Forwards 1-8, half backs 9-10, backs 11-15).

In modern times no mention of Rugby Football would be complete without the name Bill McLaren; the Scottish voice of rugby for half a century for the BBC Television coverage of Internationals. He was renowned for his thorough research, and fastidious notes, enabling his commentaries to come across wonderfully comfortable and comforting for generations of rugby viewers. Many rugby fans, who understood little of the games intricate rules, will have been brought up learning from his knowledgeable comments, and explained in that lovely gentle Borders voice. His commentaries were a master class he made the difficult seem easy. In his farewell commentary of a Six Nations Match at the Millennium Stadium Cardiff in 2002, he received a standing ovation from a 70,000 crowd. He sadly died in January 2010. In March the same year 'The Bill McLaren Foundation' was created in his memory to develop and promote the sport and its values.

With the advent of televised rugby, and the stream of new laws being introduced, a Laws Laboratory was established between the RFU and Cambridge University where utilising the college teams, they (the intelligent thinking men) could trial new laws effectively before being rolled out to the game in general. It was soon agreed that any new law should conform to three criteria: making the game safer, more enjoyable, and easier to referee. In 1976/7 the Rugby Football Union introduced proper club merit tables, but it wasn't until after the inaugural World cup in 1987, a single league structure for all the clubs in England was introduced. The success of the second World cup in 1991 alerted the money men that rugby was a valuable and desirable commodity. What many thought was merely a muddy pastime for a lot of funny people was actually an extremely valuable televisual product. The RFU finally succumbed to the inevitable, and in 1995 it turned professional. The traditions and history of many clubs and parts of the game have now gone in a rush to compete in the professional game. Outside the professional Premier league, the amateur clubs were introduced to newly formed leagues ranging from National Division one – downwards. This is the world's largest integrated sports pyramid. Nearly two hundred years after young William *'first took up the ball in his arms and ran with it'*, the game has changed beyond all recognition, but is loved the world over and big tournaments attract millions of viewers. A nation claiming the Webb Ellis Trophy is now the pinnacle of achievement in the rugby world. The annual Six-Nations tournament between, England, Scotland, Wales, Ireland, France and Italy attracts thousands of supporters and millions of old and new viewers throughout Europe.

One winter Saturday, I was making my way to the railway station with my younger brother, after an International match at Twickenham. We walked along the suburban roads from the stadium amongst the hundreds of good natured supporters, which is a constant feature and delight of the game. As we gradually shuffled towards the approaching entrance we could hear music. The crocodile queue moved nearer and we saw a group of musicals on a makeshift stand. They were entertaining us - the supporters playing a selection of popular and classic music. As we slowly passed the stand the general hubbub of conversation quietened, then a west-country voice in front spoke out *'I know that –wossit called?* Quickly and confidently another, home-counties voice from behind us replied: *'Puccini's Turandot I believe'*. Satisfied the shuffling crowd continued, glancing at each other - with unspoken understanding, we knew this could only have been experienced amongst a Twickenham crowd.

At the same stadium, amateurism is still alive and well, because the second Tuesday of December is traditionally a day when thousands of grandmothers are supposedly buried. Their imaginary funerals are the well-worn excuse for taking the afternoon off to take the train from Waterloo to Twickenham to watch the annual Varsity match between Oxford and Cambridge. This annual jamboree is not an international, nor is its appeal limited to students and graduates of the two universities themselves. For generations it is a great day out, celebrating the amateur spirit, the joyful nature of the game, and rugby's role in producing men that the country can be proud. In the car parks and bars you can meet old friends and make new ones, joined in a sense of unity for this day at least you are as one man.

There is another variation of the game which has become very popular. The Rugby Sevens. As the name suggests it's played with seven players - with just seven minutes to each half, with a one minute break, designed as a knock-out competition. It is a fun celebration of the running game and is typically a beginning or end of season tournament. It all started in the Scottish Borders in 1883 with *Melrose FC* who were casting around for ideas to help the club's finances. The idea of a tournament was posed, and it became very successful. The spectator attraction of a competitive tournament caught on and quickly spread over the 'border' into the North of England. Today, seven-a-side rugby tournaments are widely played throughout the UK.

The *Rosslyn Park National Schools Sevens* established in 1939 now attract thousands of schoolboys each year, and the popular *Middlesex (Charity) Sevens* established in 1926, played at Twickenham, is one of the country's largest sporting charities. *The Hong Kong Sevens* established in 1974, is considered a world-class event, an established party-festival in March each year, attracting clubs from around the world. Bill McLaren, in his autobiography *'Talking of Rugby'* writes at length about his Hong Kong Sevens experiences: *'I remember a big South Sea islander, saying that, in his view, the Hong Kong sevens were really the Olympic games of Rugby Union. Certainly, the Hong Kong event encapsulates all the really good things that the game has to offer —splendid organisation, wonderful sporting spirit, universal camaraderie, admirable field behaviour, the most enjoyable crowd participation, the chance for emergent rugby nations to lock horns with the mighty men of New Zealand, Australia, Wales, and the*

Barbarians offering scintillating running and handling – it's what the game is all about.' Rugby sevens is to be readmitted to the Olympics in 2016.

What may surprise is not that girls are playing rugby – but they have been since the 19th century, albeit with little publicity or much encouragement. Since the 1980's however, they have become officially organised and recognised, with founder clubs from the universities. Changing attitudes had by the 1990's made the RFU recognise their game which became part of the Rugby Football Union as the RFUW. Their game has gone from strength to strength with many countries involved in a World Cup series.

An example of the spirit of rugby is the Wooden Spoon Society, a sports charity created by English supporters after England found themselves at the bottom of the Five Nations Championship in 1983, receiving the mythical 'Wooden Spoon'. Since then they have raised millions for thousands of disadvantaged children and young people throughout the country.

When the Tsunami swept through Asia on Boxing Day 2004, many Sri Lankan Rugby players and their families were amongst its victims. It was not the damage to Asian rugby that prompted top players to respond, but the sheer scale of the disaster. Rugby players wanted to help. In March 2005 a charity match between the Northern and Southern Hemispheres, was organised, as England legend Lawrence Dallaglio said at the time *'...this match gives rugby and us players a unique opportunity...to raise a lot of money for an incredibly worthwhile cause'.* Eleven tries were scored as the South beat the North 54-19, in front of a capacity Twickenham crowd including Princes William and Harry. The money raised was staggering. The International Rugby Board (IRB) was able to hand over 3,349,943 US Dollars to the World Food Programme, the largest single donation ever received from an individual sporting event.

3. Company world of Cook's

'Far and away – the best', -

a title of a Thomas Cook long haul brochure

When I announced I was to join Thos. Cook & Son, I realised from people's reaction it conferred something of a status. It was one of the country's premier business houses and the elite travel company. Quite simply they were considered the best and thoroughly professional, a by-word for reliability. This was summed up by an advertising poster of the time *'Ask the Man from Cook's. He knows',* coupled with the old travel joke: *'If you cannot find a Cook's office, then, you are probably lost'.* This professional business ethos had developed over the years and reflected in a house style, which became the hallmark of the very best in public service. It meant that Cooks staff worked together as a business team, with little back-biting and even less back-stabbing. This *'esprit de corps'* also worked well on the playing field. Reflecting itself in a Sports Club which had been formed in 1897, quickly becoming very popular and by the early 1900's had more than 500 members.

After war-time breaks and by the time the re-constituted rugby club was formed in 1953 the company had already enjoyed over a hundred years of successful trading. The 'brand' had been well and truly established in the public's consciousness. It had weathered economic downfalls and two world wars. Providing an amazing range of services and tours, the exploits of its travellers and tours were well known and the company had become a household name as did the phrase *'Cook's Tour'.* It was the bench-mark standard for all travel companies.

Cook's had established their first London office in Ludgate Circus in 1865 gradually taking over the building, making it their Chief Office in 1873. This was a period of travel innovation as the business expanded, with Thomas Cook himself organising and leading the first round-the-world tour in 1872/3, and the Cook's Continental Timetable & Tourist Handbook published for the first time in 1873. The Cook's Circular Note –an early form of travellers cheque was launched in New York in 1874, and by 1886 his son, John Mason Cook launched his new fleet of luxurious Nile Steamers, all before the turn of the century.

Cook's first London HQ at Ludgate Circus,
home of the *Ludgate Circus Club XV* (Courtesy of TC Archives)

After the First World War, the firm had enjoyed an unprecedented period of prosperity and in 1926 it moved to a new head office in Berkeley Street in the heart of London's West End. In a new building in what had once been the garden of Devonshire House, 1,500 Cook's employees now ran the biggest office in London. In fact it was too big. For some time the 5th floor spare space was rented out to the *Pullman Car Company* which also ran the management dining-room. The display advertising of the time told the public of the change referring to its new location as *'The Temple of Travel, Berkeley Street, W1'*.

The new building contained generous amenities for staff, including a restaurant, lounge, and two recreation rooms, one for each sex. The firm also made good losses suffered by staff through the reduction of salaries in the First World War. It introduced a new pension scheme. Then in 1928 the family firm changed ownership. The remaining grandchildren of the founder, Frank and Ernest Cook sold the business to *Compagnie Internationale des Wagon-Lits et des Grands Express Européens,* operators of Europe's luxury sleeping cars including the Orient Express, for £3.5 million and retired. Whilst this was a merger of worldwide interests Cook's staff found this period difficult. Despite its international operation the company was the most British of British Institutions, it was conservative and had a civil-service style of hierarchy. It resented the intrusion of foreigners. There was even a Berkeley Street memorandum issued on the 'evils of tipping', prevalent amongst the continental staff of Wagon-Lits. Employees were told anyone accepting gratuities would be liable to instant dismissal. You still could, when I joined the company in the late 1950's.

Cooks fortunes reached their lowest ebb during World War Two, after what had by now become almost a routine operation –the rescue of British tourists from the Continent and repatriation of foreigners stranded in Britain. The firm helped take hundreds of British children to North America and Cook's became the office of the 'Children's Overseas Reception Board' in 1940. By September some 3,500 children had been taken by sea to safety in Canada, the United States and South Africa. Sadly, after the loss of over 70 children aboard the Ellerman line *'City of Benares'* sunk the same month by a U-boat in the Atlantic, the scheme was

Cook's new London HQ at Berkeley Street Mayfair,
home of *Thos Cook & Son's RFC* (Courtesy of TC Archives)

discontinued. After the fall of France the assets of
Wagon-Lits were frozen, and Thomas Cook came under
the management of Southern Railways. By 1941 Cook's
centenary year, the firm sustained a loss, and by 1942
Cook's share capital, ratified by an act of Parliament
was invested in a subsidiary company owned by the
four main line railway companies. These links were to
extend to the post war rugby section – as many games
were played against Southern, Great Western Railways
(GWR) and London, Midland & Scottish Railways (LMS)
-who also supplied and operated the Royal Train. After
the war, the Prime Minister Clement Attlee personally
prevented the firm being handed back to Wagon-Lits
despite vociferous protests from General de Gaulle.
Cook's headquarters in Berkeley Street had been
restored to its pre-war complement of around 2,000
staff. The same year, picking up where the company
had initially started in 1937, the 'School of Travel' was
founded on the 5th floor running specialized courses for
senior as well as junior staff. It was the same school
with 'Bob' Shilling as tutor that I passed through in the

early 1960's. At much the same time the railways had been nationalised and thus Thomas Cook & Son Ltd became state-owned. It took two years training to become a booking clerk in Berkeley Street, and the Travel Trade newspapers declared that most of the "chefs" in the travel business are to be found in Cook's. Other companies, which mostly made do with cheap, unskilled labour, would pay a premium to get an experienced man from Cook's into their employment. Club player Roy Bannister after de-mob in 1948 recalls the staff of the time who had worked for the company in the 1930's explaining that Head Office staff had to arrive and depart wearing 'trilby hats' – there was a staff manager on the door to ensure this. The post war travel boom continued apace and by 1950 about 2 million British holidaymakers went abroad. Over 200,000 North Americans visited the UK and 10% of them had booked through the company's overseas offices. Cook's now had a network of 350 branches in 64 countries, and its staff numbered 10,000. In Berkeley Street alone staff handled 5,000 telephone calls and 500 visitors every day. The facts are staggering. Cook's had arrangements with hundreds of shipping companies and airlines, 500 railway companies, 6,600 hotels, it issued 250,000 brochures and dealt with 7 million clients, sold £10 million and $6 million worth of travellers' cheques, and the firm's profits broke all previous records. Despite increasing competition Cook's still retained 40% of market share (remaining the largest travel agency) and record profits were running at well over £500,000 a year until the later 1950's. By 1960 Cook's had increased it Business House client accounts to 600, many of these links were forged socially on the playing fields. In 1962 Cook's first XV beat the *London French* 3-0 in their first encounter, reminding 'Mon General' of the British Government's earlier rebuff. Which he re-paid with his Gaullic 'Non', to Britain's first EEC membership application a year later. The club had established fixtures with many business 'house' teams like Fords,

Unilever, Chartered Bank, and the Foreign Office, (e.g. Pall Mall office, handled the travel arrangements for the Queen's messengers). Commercial Union, (whose rugby club closed the same year as Cook's) had experienced two of its largest insurance losses during the time we were playing against them –both travel related. In 1956 their underwriters had a heavy loss with the *Andrea Doria*, an Italian passenger vessel that collided with the *Stockholm*, a Swedish ship, some sixty miles off the USA New England coast. The ship sank within ten hours -luckily most of her passengers were saved. Then in 1963, the Glasgow to London mail train was stopped in a remote part of Buckinghamshire and £2.6 million in used notes stolen. It became known as the 'Great Train Robbery' and cost Commercial Union over a £1million. Two years later Cook's net profit exceeded £1million for the first time. However despite this business confidence, by 1965 the rugby club was in terminal decline. Why? There were a number of reasons, particularly the erosive effect of predatory staff poaching. Players like Dave Isaac joined Wakefield Fortune, as did Mike Lidbetter, Bob Maidment had already moved to a Dutch South African Bank, Hugh Dalzell joined the Italian airline Alitalia. Harry Masterton-Smith had been transferred to Cairo recalling, *'My membership of the (rugby) club was one of the key factors in my being accepted on a management training course in 1962, they felt it demonstrated a good company man!'*, and Robin Garret eventually moved on to Barclays Bank. Cook's senior management, set in their ways had an inflexible approach to these changing times. Charles Holt, who became Managing Director in 1959, was a very conservative and cautious man and like most of his peer group had risen from the clerking ranks. This created a slow career progression for many staff (dead men's shoes –an office management appointment at 40 was still considered 'young'). By the early sixties many of the original founder rugby club players (now in their thirties) had decided to 'hang up their boots' Roy Bannister had 'retired hurt' and others had disappeared. Tony Radley even emigrated to Australia to seek his fortune. Whilst some continued to play for the club as associate members, the club was finding it increasingly difficult to recruit new and committed players –particularly ones with rugby skills. This was a common complaint in other 'house' teams like Commercial Union. These events cumulated in the penultimate and disastrous 1964/5 season, when the first team lost all its recorded matches. This precipitated the end, the Rugby Union records show the last season the club was affiliated was 1965/6.

The club years 1953 – 1966
'...the times they were a changing'

The club had been re-established at a time when the post war deferential spirit of the establishment in the 1950s was gradually making way to a new age of iconoclasm. It was an era in which anything was possible and nothing was safe; a time when the established order was being challenged, subverted, and ultimately buried. This social rebellion was typically personified by the anarchic schoolgirls inspired by the drawings of Ronald Searle, in the film *The Belles of St Trinians'*, screened the season the club was revived (Any self-respecting cross-dressing rugby player would have loved the part played by Alistair Sim as Millicent Fritton the headmistress). It became a social metaphor that was amplified by the media. Then at the height of the cold war in the early 1960s, Britons paid rapt attention to a sordid little affair which involved a cabinet minister, a showgirl and a Soviet naval attaché, and it brought down the Conservative government.

The following are some of the events we lived, loved, played and enjoyed a few beers through.

1953   The cost of air travel at Easter increases by 20% on previous Easter, BOAC grounds all its *Stratocruisers* after finding an engine defect, Government plans to expand Gatwick airport, sugar & sweet rationing ends, England win Five Nations Championship, Twickenham's first 'all-ticket' match

1954   Roger Bannister runs a mile under 4 minutes, Bill Hayley's *'Rock Around the Clock'* - best selling pop record of all time, all food rationing ends, there are now 3.1 million cars in UK, Winston Churchill resigns, Boeing 707 makes its first test flight, The Anglo-Persian Oil Co. re-brands itself British Petroleum, England wins the Triple Crown, England, Wales & France share the Five Nations Championship

1955   General election –Conservatives win, Anthony Eden is Prime Minister, pint of beer 1/3d, 59% of UK men smoked, first commercial appears on television, first broadcast of BBC TV *'Dixon of Dock Green'*, with Jack Warner, Thomas Cook's amateur Operatic & Choral Society perform *'No No Nanette'*, France & Wales share the Five Nations Championship

1956   British unpopular in Egypt, riots in Cairo, British institutions set on fire: Turf club, Shepheards hotel, Cook's office, political unrest cumulating in the Suez War, Premium Bonds go on sale, first yellow 'no parking' lines appear, Prime Minister Anthony Eden resigns, BBC TV *'Whack-O'* (1956-60) school comedy series with Jimmy Edwards, British Rail abolishes third-class carriages, Wales wins the Five Nations Championship, Twickenham's original posts given to Rugby School

1957   Queen Elizabeth II makes her first televised Christmas broadcast, other popular TV programmes were *'Sunday Night at the London Palladium'* (variety 1955-68), and *'Double Your Money'* (game show 1955-68), Lewisham commuter train crash in fog killing 92, England win the 'Grand Slam' in the Five Nations Championship

1958	Eight Manchester United players die in Munich air crash, parking meters come into operation, BBC TV *'Grandstand'* sports programme first broadcast, 9,000 join first CND march to Aldermaston, Paul Raymond's Revenue Bar opens in Soho, Thomas Cook's amateur Operatic & Choral Society perform *'Call Me Madam'*, England win Five Nations Championship, the 'Penalty Try' introduced for the 1958/9 season

1959	General election, Conservatives win, Harold Macmillan is Prime Minister with a Commons majority over 100, Cook's introduces to business clients a new worldwide credit scheme for travel and related services, Cook's Brisbane office handles the travel arrangements to the UK of the Australian Rugby League 'Kangaroos' touring team, Ronnie Scott's Jazz club opens in Gerrard Street, Soho, first section of M1 motorway opened, *'The Manchester Guardian'* newspaper renamed *'The Guardian'*, post codes began to be introduced to all addresses, William Webb Ellis's grave is located at Menton on the French Riviera, Duty-Free drinks available from all British Airports, France first outright winner of the Five Nations Championship, British Lions' tour New Zealand, Australia and Canada

1960	Academy award-winning film *'The Apartment'*, Penguin prosecuted but won their case for publishing DH Lawrence's *'Lady Chatterley's Lover'*, the initial print run of 200,000 copies sold out on the day of issue, Traffic Wardens introduced in London, Hovercraft enters commercial service, UK population is now 51million, farthing coin ceases to be legal tender, Carnaby Street fashions, Mary Quant and mini-skirts, France & England share the Five Nations Championship, England wins Triple Crown

1961	George Blake, an ex-diplomat, given a record 42-year prison sentence for spying for the Russians, Berlin Wall built, the film *'West Side Story'* wins the Academy award, cash betting at betting shops made legal, satirical magazine *'Private Eye'* first published, Cambridge graduates - Alan Bennett, Peter Cook, Dudley Moore and Jonathan Miller - brought their irreverent revue, *'Beyond the Fringe'*, to London's West End, France win the Five Nations Championship

1962 *'Lawrence of Arabia'* wins Academy awards, first James Bond film; *'Dr No'*, satire on television, the late night show *'That Was The Week That Was'*, or TW3 to its aficionados, presented by David Frost, it thrived by debunking religion, politics, royalty and sex, attracting a colossal audience of 12million viewers, Beatles first record, Cuban Missile crisis, Thomas Cook's amateur Operatic & Choral Society perform *'The Vagabond King'* at King George's Hall, France win the Five Nations Championship, British Lions' tour South Africa

1963 Charles de Gaulle vetos Britain's entry to the EEC, Academy award -winning film *'Tom Jones'*, 'Beeching report' –begins rail closures, Kim Philby named as 'third man', the Great Train Robbery, £2.6m stolen, President Kennedy assassinated, Christine Keeler jailed (Profumo affair), the Prime Minister Harold McMillan resigns, Beatles first No 1 hit *'from me to you'*, England win the Five Nations Championship

1964 General election Labour win and Harold Wilson becomes Prime Minister (they had been out of office since 1951), Academy award-winning film *'My Fair Lady'*, Radio Caroline starts transmission, there are now 8.4m cars in UK, the weekly wage £13.9s.6d, 54% men and 41% women smoked, Parliament votes to abolish capital punishment, Scotland & Wales share the Five Nations Championship

1965 Pint of beer 1/9d, Ronnie Scott's Jazz club moves to Frith Street Soho, Winston Churchill dies aged 90 (State funeral), Academy award -winning film *'The Sound of Music'*, cigarette ads. banned on TV, 70 mph speed limit introduced, Mini Cooper cost

£679, Thomas Cook's profit exceeded £1m for the first time, Ian Smith and the White Rhodesians declare UDI, Wales wins the Five Nations Championship, and Triple Crown

1966   Academy award -winning film *'A Man For All Seasons',* Harold Wilson, Prime Minister, the Labour Government re-imposed the £50 travel allowance -remaining in force till 1970, Aberfan disaster, (116 children and 28 adults lost their lives in Welsh coal-tip landslide), Wales wins the Five Nations Championship

The club's demise also coincided with the anarchic schoolgirls last appearance in *'The Great St Trinians' Train Robbery'* in 1966. However, it wasn't all gloom, the same year the company celebrated its 125th anniversary, and England was hosting and winning the world Cup at Wembley. But then the bad news, Harold Wilson's new Labour government re-imposed the £50 travel allowance – hitting Cook's business hard, more than most, as around a third of the firm's tours fell beyond the limit. It was losing the competitive edge and a new international trend was developing, with financial groups like Thomson moving into the industry. The company was slowly reorganising and moving away from 'state ownership'. By the early 1970's Thomas Cook was privatised and bought by a consortium led by the Midland Bank (now HSBC). The advertising company McCann Erickson was employed to revamp the firm's image resulting in a new box logo in 'flaming red' changing the name to Thomas Cook (the *'& Son'* disappeared altogether). By 1977 it moved its Berkeley Street Head Office to a new administrative headquarters at Thorpe Wood in Peterborough, the London era was over.

However, the ever resilient Thomas Cook with its worldwide brand has prospered. By 1989 profits had reached £22.5 million and by 2005 Thomas Cook UK & Ireland announces its greatest ever profits of £50 million. Cook's had outgrown Thorpe Wood and moved into the Thomas Cook Business Park a few miles away. A year later the company announces record profits of £83.3 million and achieves the 'holy grail' of the travel industry, a five per cent profit margin. Thomas Cook is also listed as one of the Sunday Times Top 20 Best big companies to work for. In the summer of 2007 Thomas Cook becomes part of Thomas Cook plc which was formed by the merger of Thomas Cook AG and MyTravel Group plc. Thomas Cook Group plc is today a global brand with a network of more than 3,400 stores across 21 countries and over 22.3 million customers, and 19,000 staff, making it one of the world's leading leisure groups. The name features amongst the Top 500 'Consumer Superbrands'.

The company story continues and as they now say, 'Don't just book it. Thomas Cook it'.

The Thomas Cook Business Park Coningsby Road, Bretton, Peterborough

4. Cook players - part one & two (1910 - 1939)
Ludgate Circus XV / Thos. Cook & Son's RFC

'The dirtier his shorts, the better he plays,'
-a reference to the club's scrum half, 1925/6 season

The original rugby section was formed in 1910 and was known as the Ludgate Circus Club XV with its first mention in the Ludgate Circus Club Magazine (early staff magazine) in September 1911 featuring a short report of the club's first season.

"Although only started last year, this section has already been very hard hit by losing some of its best men, who have been transferred or have left the service. Messrs. Bayliss, Crawley, Biddell, Lansberry and Foster are notable losses, whose excellent play will be severely missed. Yet we have many stalwarts left who will carry the Club colours this season with distinction, and, with the talent still to be discovered amongst the new members who have joined, we anticipate another good season. We have before us this season possibly harder contests than have been experienced, but where there's a will there's a way". The article goes on to say, R. G. Smithard the Honorary Secretary, will be only too pleased to give all the necessary information to aspiring candidates for this strenuous game, and it is hoped that many will come forward and make this section as popular as it was last year. A splendid fixture list has been arranged and many enjoyable games should result. The practice games will shortly start, and he who runs may learn and is sure of receiving a very hearty welcome to the "Rugger" fold.

Rugby ceased during the war years of 1914 to 1918 and it wasn't until 1921 that the club was re-established. At that time the club's officials used to summarise each season's activities with players' strengths and weaknesses in an article in the staff magazine –by now re-titled *'The Globe Trotter'*- it was really like a house master's report. At the end of the 1923/4 season we learn in the April issue, that B.E.

Groom (like vintage wine) improves steadily, and that W.G. Trend is a brilliant forward, but should remember that kicking 'is' allowed, (taking that on-board) he became captain two seasons later. Also J E Wright described as a dashing forward, should really learn that his paramount job is to 'shove'. Whilst we read that F.D.W Roach is an excellent scrummager, but likes a rest after a scrum!

The Ludgate Circus Club XV 1923/4 season

'The Globe Trotter' Magazine July 1924 (Courtesy of TC Archives) *Back Row:* J. Burgess, A. Moves, A. Copson, A.C. Johns, J. Warden, H. Monk, R.H. Roach, S. Bates, J.E. Murray, F.J. Floyd, *Front Row:* L.C. Pettitt, B.E. Groom, G.E. Gambling, E.D. Murrell (Capt.), E.J. Hill, H. Lawrence, A.P. Wilson *(Note: A Copson and E D Murrell (Capt) are wearing their 'Honours Cap' awarded at the end of season annual rugby section dinner)*

By the end of 1925/6 season in the August issue they were listed under the heading "*Who's Who*" by N.M.S. – the initials of the Chairman of committee, who was also a touch judge. It was a period when only first name initials were published, so we have to speculate as to what they might be known as. It provides amusing reading.

The season of 1925/6

Name/position	N.M.S. comments
F.C. Lloyd (Full Back)	Usually a safe and sound kicker and good touch finder, but sometimes apt to suffer from nerves. Rather inconsistent.
W.W.G. Houghton (Full Back)	With a little more experience should develop into a good back. Fairly safe tackle and good kick.
R.F. Kerr (R.W. Three-quarter)	Has made rapid strides this season, which augurs well for next year. His speed is invaluable asset to the side.
J. Tyerman (L.C. Three-quarter)	Secretary of the section. Does as good work for the side off the field as on, which is saying a very great deal. Absolutely invaluable.
F. Curtis	Puts his heart and soul into the game. A great asset to the team who plays for "Rugger's sake".
F.P.R. Dunwoich (L.W. Three-quarter)	A very promising three-quarter, who should develop into a really good winger.
E.J.K. Higgins (R.C. Three-quarter)	In a few years should be a really first-class player. A splendid tackler and always does the right thing at the right moment. Thoroughly deserves his cap.
A.P. Wilson (Scrum Half)	One of the hardest workers on the field. Does not give the opposing half breathing space. The dirtier his shorts, the better he plays.
R.T. Hughes (Stand-off Half)	Has done a lot of good work and great things are expected of him next season.

W. Trend (Forward) & Capt.	The right man in the right place. A tremendous worker and excellent leader.
L.C. Pettitt (Forward)	A forward we could not afford to do without. A very good dribbler.
R. Coussens (Forward)	Never stops from start to finish; a splendid forward and thoroughly deserves his cap.
G.S. Dodd (Forward)	Another "non-stop," who puts his whole heart into the game. Deserves a cap.
H. Graves (Forward)	An excellent hooker. Uses his weight to advantage and always gives a good account of himself.
P.J. White (Forward)	A really good player who is rapidly making himself indispensable.
H.W. Lamb (Forward)	A good forward, who can also acquit himself well at three-quarter.
H.K. Ryper (Forward)	A good forward, but would like to see him use his weight a little more.
R.H. Stokes (Forward)	A very promising player who should develop rapidly later on.
F.E. Crome (Forward)	A useful player, but rather on the small side. Always tries his best.

The staff magazine records that in the 1925/6 season the Club XV played 19 games - 10 wins, 8 lost and 1 drawn. The report goes on to say *'Undoubtedly the game of the season was that in which a St. Bart's (Bartholomew's) Hospital team were met in aid of the Hospital Comforts Fund. After a very hard game we were beaten by one try to nil (3-0), and that scored in the very last minute of the first half. Although justice was no doubt served by the result, the Club played an exceedingly good game and can be congratulated on a very plucky and praiseworthy display.'* (Bart's had won the Hospitals Cup the previous year). The end of season dinner was held and 'Honour Caps' awarded (these were voted by player consensus). *The 'Globe Trotter'* magazine also reports that one of the players (we now learn his first name) Frank Curtis, married at the end of the season in April (how thoughtful of him), and a wedding gift was presented by the Rugger section of *'a blue Wedgwood china biscuit barrel –suitably inscribed'.* It ends with the section plan to endeavour to run two fifteens in the following season. Things were looking up. However, the next decade found the inevitable war clouds looming, and the Government introducing a national military 'call up' of eligible young men. By end of season 1938/9 the rugby section had been disbanded. Curiously, the RFU records show the club's affiliation as being 1926/7 to 1931/2.

Some players of the Ludgate Circus Club XV

This was the name of the club from its inception in 1910 until 1926, when it was renamed Thos. Cook & Son's RFC. Very little is known about the players other that what was briefly published in various club reports featured in staff magazines, *'Ludgate Circus Club Magazine'* and later *The Globe Trotter'* between, 1911 and 1928. These are some of them.

Name	**Seasons played, position, awarded 'Honours Cap'**
Bates, S	1923/4
Bayliss,	Original founder player 1910/1 season
Biddell,	Original founder player 1910/1 season
Burgess, J	1923/4
Copson, A	1923/4 *'Honours Cap'*
Coussens, R	Forward, 1925/6, awarded *'Honours Cap'* 1925/6
Crawley,	Original founder player 1910/1 season

Crome, F.E.	Forward, 1925/6
Curtis, F (Frank)	1925/6
Dodd, G.S.	Forward, 1925/6
Dunwoich, F.P.R.	Left wing three-quarter, 1925/6
Dunworth, P.R.	Awarded 'Honours Cap' 1927/8
Floyd, F.J.	1923/4
Foster,	Original founder player 1910/1 season
Gambling, G.E.	Scrum half, 1923/4
Graves, H	Hooker, 1925/6
Groom, B.E.	Centre, 1923/4
Higgins, E.J.K.	Right centre three-quarter, 1925/6 *'Honours Cap'*
Hill, E.J.	1923/4
Houghton, W.W.G.	Full Back, 1925/6
Hughes, R.T.	Stand-off half, 1925/6
Johns, A.C.	Full Back, 1923/4, awarded *'Honours Cap'*
Kerr, R.F.	Right wing three-quarter, 1925/6
Lamb, H.W.	Forward, 1925/6
Lansberry,	Original founder player 1910/1 season
Lawrence, H.	1923/4
Lloyd, F.C.	Full Back, 1925/6
Monk, H.	Forward, 1923/4
Moves, A	1923/4
Moyes, A	1923/4
Murray, J.F.	Forward, 1923/4
Murrell, E.D.	Captain, 1923/4, Forward, awarded *'Honours Cap' Capt '23/4*
Perrett Young, J.G.C	Referee, 1925/6, *(Lon. Soc. of RU referees)* Club Hon. Sec. 1927 (Rates Dept)
Pettitt, L.C.	1923/4, Forward 1925/6,
Pinder, W.J.	*Vice Captain, 1923/4*, all-rounder
Roach, F.D.W.	Forward, 1923/4
Roach, R.H.	1923/4
Ryper, H.K.	Forward, 1925/6
Smithard, R.G.	Hon Sec. 1911/2
Smith, N.M. (Murray)	Hon. Sec. 1923/4, Committee chairman, 1925/6
Stokes, R.H.	Forward, 1925/6

Trend, W.G.	Forward, 1923/4, awarded *'Honours Cap', Capt.1925/6,*
Tyreman, J.	1923/4, left centre three-quarter, 1925/6
Warden, J.	Wing, 1923/4
White, P.J.	Forward, 1925/6, awarded *'Honours Cap'* 1927/8
Wilson, A.P.	Wing, 1923/4, scrum half 1925/6
Wright, J. E.	Forward, 1923/4

From French kissing to the Home Guard

The club played against a background of tumultuous social, political and travel events that were to shape the following thirty years. The 1911 census showed a country with a population of 40.8 million, the weekly wage of a train driver was £2 0s 6d and a pint of beer cost 3d, same as a copy of *'The Times'*, and the inland letter postage rate was 1d. Bernard Shaw's new play *Pygmalion* was a West End success, and by 1919 Thos Cook & Son was the first travel agent to advertise pleasure trips by air.

1910   First time an air passenger is flown across the channel, King Edward VII dies, Dr Crippen hanged in London for poisoning his wife, kissing banned on French trains after claims that prolonged farewells delay trains, this year for the first time France was included with the original 'four' Nations Rugby Competition, England won, and the competition now called the 'Five Nations Championships, Twickenham staged its first international match, England beating Wales, 11-6, the first British Lions' tour to South Africa

1911   The first Monte Carlo Rally takes place, Coronation of George V, First electric trolley-buses appear, Suffragettes riot in Whitehall, Wales won the Five Nations Championship

1912   *'Titanic'* sinks after hitting an iceberg, with a loss of 1513 lives, National Insurance introduced, Captain Scott dies on way back from South Pole, England and Ireland shared the Five Nations Championship

1913   Charlie Chaplin makes his first film, the Panama Canal opens linking the Atlantic and Pacific oceans, 10mph speed limit at Hyde Park corner-world's busiest road junction, England won the Five Nations Championship

1914-1918 World War One – fought against Germany, during this period, photo's were introduced for the first time in British passports, passenger liner *'Lusitania'* torpedoed, loss of 1198 lives, the first air raid on London, nurse Edith Cavell shot by Germans, the Women's Institute founded, and the Royal Air Force formed.
This great war saw the irrevocable lost of at least 67 rugby internationals from the four home countries.

1919   First daily international mail and passenger flights between Paris and London are introduced, first meeting of the League of Nations in Paris

The Twenties: By 1921 the population of Great Britain was 42.7 million, and by 1923 you would have paid 10d for 8 *Players No.3 cigarettes* and £175 for a 2-seater *Morris Cowley*, by the end of the decade a radio licence cost 10s 0d., the film *The Jazz Singer* was a hit (the first full-length 'talking' film), the fox-trot dance was popular. In the USA Thos Cook & Son organised the first personally-conducted air tour from New York to Chicago in 1927 for the Tunney -Dempsey II heavyweight boxing contest, (Gene Tunney won).

1920   A new airmail service starts to Amsterdam costing 3d per ounce of mail, Oxford University awards degrees to women, a night bus service starts in

London, after the 'Treaty of Trianon' – several new states come into being, Hungary, Czechoslovakia & Yugoslavia, England, Scotland and Ireland shared the Five Nations Championship

1921 British Legion holds its first 'Poppy Day', record numbers of people travel on the 50th anniversary of the August bank holiday, 'town full' notices are put up in Blackpool, England won the Five Nations Championship

1922 *Thomas Cook & Son* organises the first tour to cover the whole length of the African continent, lasting five months, including a one-month safari, Queen Mary opens Waterloo station, 'Austin Seven', the first British car for the popular market introduced, Civil Aviation Advisory Board is established, Wales won the Five Nations Championship

1923 The first 24-hour Le Mans Grand Prix is won by a Frenchman, First FA Cup final held at Wembley, England won the Five Nations Championship

1924 *Thomas Cook & Son Ltd is incorporated*, Imperial Airways is established with a fleet of 13 aircraft flying from Croydon, First Labour Government voted to power, USSR recognised by British Government, England won the Five Nations Championship

1925 The Ministry of Transport decides to paint white lines on Britain's roads in an attempt to reduce accidents, Daylight saving becomes a permanent institution, Scotland won the Five Nations Championship

1926 *The Ludgate Circus Club XV changed its name to Thos. Cook & Son's RFC,* John Logie Baird, gives first public demonstration of television, German airline Lufthansa is founded, the first General Strike in British history, Ireland and Scotland shared the Five Nations Championship

1927   Transatlantic telephone service between London and New York opens, the first scheduled London – Delhi flight arrives in India after a 63-hour flight, Ireland and Scotland shared the Five Nations Championship

1928   The 'Flying Scotsman' train makes the first non-stop journey from London to Edinburgh, Alexander Fleming discovers Penicillin, Piccadilly Circus tube station opens, England won the Five Nations Championship

1929   The Graf Zeppelin flies around the world in 21 days, trial flight of British airship R101, it is announced that London buses will be red, after yellow-and-red prove unpopular, Scotland won the Five Nations Championship

The Thirties: In 1931 the population had grown to 44.7 million. By 1935 the typical weekly pay-packet of a clerical worker was £3 13s 10d but that of a coal miner £2 4s 8d, a pint of beer cost 7d and a bottle of *Gordon's Gin* 12s 6d. *Players Navy Cut* cigarettes cost 6d and a *Mars Bar* 2d. People were singing *'On the Sunny Side of the Street'* and going to the theatre to see Noel Coward's *'Private Lives'*.

1930   Amy Johnson makes her solo flight to Australia, the Highway code is introduced, the R101 airship crashes en route to India killing over 40 people, England won the Five Nations Championship, the first Lions' tour to New Zealand and Australia

1931   First 33⅓ rpm long-playing records, Gandhi visits London, Imperial Airways starts a new route connecting London with Central Africa, Wales won the five nations championship

1932   'Instant Coffee' first sold in Britain, First 'Crazy Gang' show opens in London, Imperial Airways begins regular service between London and Cape Town, England, Wales, Ireland share the Five Nations Championship

1933   Two British planes are first to fly over Mount Everest, the Boeing 247 becomes the first modern-style airliner, Air France is created, Adolf Hitler appointed German Chancellor, Scotland won the Five Nations Championship

1934   Cunard-White Star ocean liner *SS Queen Mary* launched, Yorkshireman Percy Shaw patents the 'Cats eye' road stud, Pedestrian crossings are introduced in London, England won the Five Nations Championship

1935   First Penguin paperbacks go on sale, Silver Jubilee of King George V, driving tests become compulsory in Britain, GPO telegram service introduced, Ireland won the Five Nations Championship

1936   King Edward VII abdicates, 'speaking clock' introduced by GPO, a new Night Train ferry is established Dover-Dunkirk –passengers don't have to leave their sleeping cars, Wales won the Five Nations Championship

1937   Billy Butlin opens his first holiday camp at Skegness, nearly 150,000 watch football match between England and Scotland, first London Motor Show opens at Earl's Court, England won the Five Nations Championship

1938   Nazi Germany invaded Austria, the 'Holidays With Pay Act' comes into force allowing more people to travel at home and abroad, The steam train *'Mallard'* achieved 126mph on Sunday 3rd July, a world record, Gas masks issued to school children, Scotland won the Five Nations Championship, the second British Lions' tour to South Africa

1939   Imperial Airways merge with British Airways forming BOAC, Cook's and LMS Railway build and open Prestatyn Holiday Camp *(a more up-market version of Butlins, promoted as 'The Chalet Village*

by the Sea'), BBC 'Home Service' begins, Hitler invades Poland starting World War Two, England, Ireland, Wales share the Five Nations Championship

1940 The *SS 'Queen Elizabeth'* makes her maiden voyage to the USA in secret, Winston Churchill becomes Prime Minister, allied forces are evacuated from Dunkirk by the Royal Navy and a fleet of 'little' ships, the RAF win the Battle of Britain, Food rationing starts, Home Guard formed

World War Two 1939 – 1945 saw the loss of at least 39 rugby internationals from the four home counties. Ireland alone (whilst remaining a neutral country in that conflict) lost 7 internationals fighting for the allied cause.

'The Experienced traveller takes his bank with him'
'The wise traveller has friends everywhere'
(poster images courtesy of TC Archives)

5. Cook players - part three (1953 - 1966)
Thos. Cook & Son's RFC

'...Merry, merry men are we,
'because there's none so fair as can compare with the TCRFC'
club chorus of *'Old King Cole',* (Rugby version)

After the war with returning National Service personnel provided a stimulus to create a revival in the company rugby club. This was led by a group from the Post Order Department in Berkeley Street including Don Keston, Roy Dangerfield the Captain and Alex Down who set about their recruitment campaign. Again the *Cook's Staff magazine* was used to spread the word. The interest it created allowed a team to be formed for the 1953/4 season. Roy Bannister, who had joined the company a few years earlier from National Service with the RAF, was one of the founder team members, and recalls being invited to *The Goat Tavern* in Stafford Street, (through a narrow alleyway from Berkeley Street) to hear about the team plans. One of the organisers who will remain nameless, through some unfortunate company fraud or embezzlement was later sentenced to a period of detention at Ford Open Prison in Sussex. He apparently would occasionally appear at away games – but of course at the home ground in Ravensbourne he was 'persona non grata'. Roy remembers *'we lost the first couple of games heavily, but gradually got better'*.

We were all part of a very British firm, despite its international operation the company was at the time rather conservative and had a civil-service style of hierarchy. The company staff was widely diverse but seemed to work together as a team, as it did on the playing field. Many staff had seen active service during the war, and others in National Service would delight in the quiet subversion of authority. Although they were thoroughly professional, some also delightfully individual eccentrics that would not be out of place in an Ealing comedy. For example, during a particularly energetic leg-sapping match one of the team who will remain nameless, on receiving the ball, kicked it deep into touch, in fact so deep it took ages to find the ball. There didn't seem to be a tactical reason for the kick, and I can recall asking him why he did it, *'I needed a smoke'* was his laconic reply. Inside his shorts revealed a small pocket containing a cigarette butt and a book of matches, courtesy of *Murray's Cabaret Club*. (This Soho club is where Christine Keeler and Mandy Rice Davies the sex scandal girls linked to the *'Profumo Affair'* worked).

Thos Cook & Son's Sports Club was established in 1897 – but was then known as the *'Ludgate Circus Athletic Club'*, when the existing football and swimming clubs amalgamated. The new club had four sections – football, swimming, cricket and tennis – and the playing facilities scattered across London. Despite having no ground, it proved popular and by 1902 the club was simply known as the *'Ludgate Circus Club'*. A year later a suitable site was identified at Ravensbourne in Kent. Thomas Cook's grandsons, Frank and Ernest bought the site and laid the ground and erected a pavilion, and by 1905 it had become one of the finest private athletic grounds near London. It provided two football pitches during the winter and four tennis courts, two cricket pitches and a bowling green during the summer. The same year it hosted the first 'garden party'. In 1910 the rugby section was formed and a sports day was inaugurated which became the forerunner of this annual event each year. By the summer of 1911 the membership had reached 600, and other sections had been introduced including running (harriers) chess and draughts, bowls, shooting (rifle range) and cycling. The First World War brought an end to sporting activities for six years. A new pavilion was built at Ravensbourne in 1922 which was opened in June by the Club's President, Frank Cook, the grandson of Thomas. The 1920's were a period of remarkable success with sections winning many cups and awards and the launch of the new operatic section staged its first production of Gilbert and Sullivan's *HMS Pinafore* in November 1924. A year later the dramatic section staged its first play. One of the consequences of the move to new head office premises in Berkeley Street in 1926 was a name change. The club became known as *Thos. Cook & Son's Sports Club*. The post war President of the Sports Club at the time the rugby club was Sir John Elliot (who had been Cook's chairman since 1959) and the overall club's Honorary Secretary was A.J. (Andy) Anderson, who had travelled to Hilversum in 1958 as an observer. The club continued until the mid 1970's when the company relocated their headquarters to Peterborough. The final sports day was staged in July 1975. The club survived these social upheavals and relocation changes, and today, with the emphasis placed on social events the club was renamed *Thomas Cook Sports and Social Club*. The annual Ravensbourne sports day tradition survives in a new format. Today in its new location in Peterborough it has grown in popularity to become known as the *'National Annual Family Gathering'* with the company hosting a lunch creating a social opportunity to catch up with former colleagues and friends.

The people that made it happen
Club officials 1953 – 1966

No amateur club can function without the enthusiastic commitment of officials who work in an honorary capacity. Behind the scenes they make things happen. In the rugby section we had the successor of the dedicated *Ludgate Circus Club* officials in Derek Bascombe. He had to liaise with the games governing bodies – the rugby section was affiliated both to the *Kent County Rugby Football Union* and the *Rugby Union.* He and a small band of colleagues arranged suitable fixtures by phone, personal contact or attending one of the ad hoc fixture forums in central

London pubs, securing games over the winter seasons, and through other committees generally administered the functions that make games possible. Naturally, they also held down their company jobs too. These people and their tireless spirit did much to establish the post war revival of Thos. Cook & Son's rugby club. The Club re-launched in 1953 with Roy Dangerfield as Captain, Alex Down initially as Secretary, and Derek Bascombe writing club promotions pieces in the Staff Magazine from 1954 onwards. During the late 1950's through to the mid 1960's a group of names consistently appear in club records like; (the diminutive) Derek Bascombe, who often refereed our games, as he was also a member of the *Kent Society of Rugby Football Union Referee's* - a skill he took on the first club tour to Hilversum in 1958 (see photos). Hugh Dalzell as the Honorary Match Secretary arranged our fixture list for both First and 'A' teams, and for a time also captained the First XV. Gary Mos, who played against the Hilversum visitors in 1960, also looked after the club's finances and player subscriptions as the Honorary Treasurer. In addition to these responsibilities, they also played in matches – some eventually retiring from the game in the early 1960's.

The kit and caboodle of the game

The club colours were royal blue, gold and chocolate. These were presented as a royal blue jersey set with a wide gold hoop, flanked top and bottom with a narrow chocolate key line, and white collar. The pattern was similar for the socks, with navy blue shorts. The club colours seemed to have been unchanged since 1910, although there was an alternative 'A' XV strip see photos. As with any amateur team we bought our own kit. The appointed supplier was an old family firm and '*the*' sports outfitters Messrs. Lillywhites of Piccadilly Circus, a short walk from Cook's head-office. The shop was originally established in the Haymarket in 1863 moving to the beautiful early Victorian building on the edge of Piccadilly Circus in 1925. The shop has attracted the greatest sportsmen, celebrities and royalties (once a Royal Warrant Holder) for well over a century. Unrivalled in its service and quality, the shop was a quintessential working example of an old English department store, as it is a place to buy sporting goods. The business had been built by a keen cricketing family. The shop's founder James Lillywhite,  captained the England XI playing the very first test match in Australia. Over six vast floors they supplied everything a rugby player needed, like boots, *'with extra studs, always useful sir', socks of course, and shorts, -in navy blue? Umbro are the best, sir'*. *'Of course sir will need an athlete's support, or as some of my 'northern' gentlemen clients refer to it as a 'jockstrap'*. These were manufactured by Litesome Sportswear of Keighley Yorkshire, (swimming trunks were an alternative). Around the corner from Lillywhites in Piccadilly Circus was a Boots 'all-night' chemist, *'where sir could buy the usual athlete's requisites, like Elliman's Universal Embrocation, 'I believe its widely used as a pre-sport rub on muscles especially in winter Sir'*. In reality of course, the players presented themselves with a medley of kit (see photos) with a variety of different styles, various coloured shorts, and a mixture of socks that would not look out of place in a *Barbarians* team. This was to become a benefit to me in later seasons. Playing at scrum-half for the 'A' team, I could easily see the hooker Dave Keeling's high visibility red socks, amongst the legs in the 'steaming' scrum, on grey misty winter afternoons. In the amateur game fixtures were arranged in an ad hoc and informal way. Usually if one club had played another club, they would, if agreeable arrange to play them again the following season. This would fill many fixtures during a September to April season but inevitably there would be gaps. So from time to time there would be a 'fixture exchange'. As Roy Bannister recalls, fixture secretaries and club members would get together informally from time to time, usually in central London pubs. Hugh Dalzell explained these would take place about twice a year at the *Phoenix* pub near Oxford Circus on the corner of Margaret Street and Cavendish Square. They would meet other rugby contacts wishing to arrange fixtures between their respective clubs. It would be organised by a Metropolitan Police sergeant with an encyclopaedic knowledge of the clubs, who could always suggest likely fixtures. This seemed to work. If chosen to play – the team Captain would send a 'selection slip' through the internal Cook's mail system (Pall Mall office had uniformed messengers to collect mail from Berkeley Street, -it also had a convenient basement boiler room with hot pipes for unofficially drying rugby kit).

Cook's XV, Ravensbourne c.1957 ('old style' jerseys)

(Photo Hugh Dalzell)
Standing *left to right*: (☺?), (☺?), Ivor Jenkins, (☺?), Fred Jenkins, Pete Dawson?, (☺?), (☺?), (☺?), Kneeling *left to right:* Vic Bulmer-Jones, Gary Mos, Ralph Knowles, Don Keston, Freddie Petts, Derek Sells

This was a pre-typed slip with hand-written details giving team, playing position and travelling instructions of where the opposition club was located – and sometimes a group meeting point often outside a pub. A few members I recall had the word 'outside' underlined as a personal instruction. The company supported the Sports Club but each player had to pay a subscription. We of course paid our own travelling costs, beer kitty contributions (the enamel jug –see photo) and sometimes additional catering for our visitors like occasionally half pints of shandies in their changing room. One of the benefits being

Thos Cook & Son's 'A' XV team 1960/1 season, Ravensbourne
Sunday 8th January 1961,
before annual match with 'First' team (lost 0 -18 pts)
Standing left to right: Robin Garrett, Mike Lakin, Colin McRitchie, Geoff Brooks, Don Keston (Capt), Pete Simmons, Pete Robertson, Jim Collett, *Sitting left to right:* Bill Trenfield, Gerry Silk, Vic Bulmer-Jones, Bobbie Gould, Romeo Bazzali, John Dann, L. Samson *('A' XV wearing alternative old club jerseys')*

affiliated to the Rugby Union (the word 'football' was added later), meant the club was entitled to apply for international tickets for matches at Twickenham. I recall seeing many matches including the 1963

Calcutta Cup match from the old South Stand with my fiancé, who after hours of standing unfortunately fainted during the second half, but was helpfully carried by supportive spectators through the crowd to the St John Ambulance station under the stand to recover. (If you are wondering, England won 10-8).

Rugby like the travel industry embraces a wide diversity of like minded people and the club included a mixture of players of different back grounds, schools and countries stretching from the English Home Counties and beyond. Their ages ranged from mid-teens to mid thirties, some married with families –some single, but with a common bond in the love of rugby. Many had played at school, or the Forces some had never played before! Most players were English but as seems traditional in many rugby clubs the odd few Welshmen make an appearance, like Brian and George Davies. The Scots represented by Colin McRichie and Ian McKenzie (who worked in the Press Office), and an Irishman Colin McCarthy (a smiling good natured colleague, when we toured Holland together), cover the requisite sample of the club's home nations representatives. From overseas we had (our fleet-footed) Jim Munnick, a black South African who was appointed Vice-Captain of the 'A' XV for the 1964/5 season. Roy Butcher recalls another South African who played for a short time with the club, and quickly earned the epithet 'shirt-ripper' because of the amount of times he would tear opposition jerseys in tackles, seemingly needlessly, creating complaints from opposition captains. (Remember, we had to buy our own shirts). He shrugged this off with a dismissive view of the differences between South African and English rugby as *'you (the English) play to exercise -whilst we (South Africans) exercise to play'*. Romeo Bazzali of Italian decent usually played Full Back, and used to drive a Sunbeam Rapier car, at a time when most of us travelled by public transport. There was Jurek (Rocky to his team-mates) Rokosvinski, a young, 'tall and hard' Polish player who later went on to join the

Swinton Rugby League club, and soon to be exiled Harry Masterton-Smith who after a few seasons was sent to Cook's Cairo office. We had expatriates like Steve Sutcliffe-Hey who had been in the Merchant Navy in the Far East, before returning to the UK. Some of us (the single 'A' XV players) used enjoy riotous after game parties in his house, There were others who had served National Service, like Don Keston (Royal Navy), who reminded me many times he'd once played for Penarth in Wales, Mike Lidbetter (Royal Engineers at Suez), Robin Garrett (RAF) Biggin Hill, Derek Sells (RAF) in the Middle East, as was Roy Bannister, who recalls his introduction to rugby, *'I was minding my own business one day sunning myself in about 135°F in Habbanyia an RAF station just west of Baghdad, when along came an 'erk' (RAF vernacular for a ground crew) and said 'you'll do'.* Vic Bulmer-Jones too had been in the RAF (with moustache to prove it).

Cook's 1ˢᵗ XV, Ravensbourne, Season 1961/2   (Photo Mike Lakin)
Standing left to right: (☺?), (☺?) Gerry Silk, Roy Butcher, Jim Munnick, Hugh Dalzell, (☺?), Jurek (Rocky) Rokosvinski, (☺?), (☺?), *Sitting left to right*: Romeo Bazzali, Bob Maidment, Dave Isaac (with ball), Marcus Wade (with 'Beatle' style haircut), Bill Trenfield

Some players also enjoyed other field sports, like Brian Wright who (when not chasing and capturing the prettiest girls), was ensuring the next round was on our opponents by unerringly hitting the finishing doubles on the dart board. He also played Hockey for Cook's and George Davies played association football for a Sunday team. *The Goat Tavern* in Stafford Street became home to many of the Foreign Exchange people during the winter off-season. If not on 'departmental relief' they would while away their time over 'three hour' lunches. Berkeley Street at that time had around 2,000 personnel and was naturally the source of many players such as Don Keston, Derek Sells and Gary Mos, from the Post Order Department (POD), Hugh Dalzell from Holiday Tours (HTD), Conducted Tours (CTD) provided Mike Lakin, Gerry Silk and Bill Trenfield, whilst Passports provided Vic Bulmer-Jones and the Press Office Ian McKenzie. The Foreign Exchange (FE) departments provided George Halliday, Roy Butcher, Dave Dowling and Dave Keeling. The London offices supplied others like Mike Lidbetter (Kensington High St.), John Carter (Leadenhall St.), Roy Bannister (Harrods) and the author (Pall Mall).

Beginning of 1963/64 season – Thos Cook & Son's 'A' XV
Top left to right: (☺?),(☺?), Robin Garrett, Tony Radley, Roy Butcher, Derek Sells (V.Capt), (☺?), (☺?), *Bottom left to right:* (☺?), (☺?), John Dann, Mike Lakin (Capt), Dave Keeling, Vic Bulmer-Jones, (note the variety of jersey's, shorts & socks –and there are only 14 players).

Some team player sketches

Some players appeared for just a few matches, whilst others for seasons. This is a selection of remembered players and officials of the club. It could be a typical Cook's 'A' XV as it has only fourteen players and a referee. As with many rugby clubs there are the *non-conformists* which in our case was manifest by wearing 'white' shorts as apposed to 'house' colour navy blue.

Roy Bannister - one of the Club's founder players, recruited in *The Goat Tavern* in 1953. He had joined the company in the autumn of 1948 after National Service in Iraq with the RAF, where he learnt his rugby. Amongst his many roles was working as relief manager in some London offices, including Harrods, Holborn and the House of Commons. He was a forward and a member of the first tour to Holland in 1958, but had his career tragically cut short with a serious injury. He was the first (and thankfully the only) player to break his neck when a scrum collapsed during a Sunday match in March 1960, playing against a Foreign Exchange (Forex) side at Ravensbourne. He was taken to a cottage hospital in Beckenham in Hugh Dalzell's minivan; then to Farnborough hospital in a 'real' ambulance, with the doctor advising the driver to avoid pot-holes. After three months followed by twelve months convalescing he recovered. On the bright side he did meet his future wife Bridget who had nursed him in hospital. Luckily Harry Masterton-Smith was on hand to book their honeymoon trip –that's rugby teamwork! Now an octogenarian, he still enjoys cycling, walking and acting as a 'Marshall' for his local cycling club rallies in Hertfordshire.

Derek Bascombe - a stalwart to the post war reconstituted club and one of the founder members. He was Honorary Secretary, and was affiliated to the Kent Society of Referees. He wrote many recruitment pieces for the staff magazine, and refereed many home matches. This was a skill he took on tour to Hilversum in 1958, where he refereed some of the tour matches. He has to my knowledge actually played in a match when we were 'short' of a player. Typically, post match he'd be seen in the midst of club activities with a 'jug' of beer doing the rounds in the bar at Ravensbourne. Harry Masterton-Smith remembers *'he also kept good control of the beer kitty when carried over from one match to the next'*. Roy Bannister recalls an incident on the first Hilversum tour, when the touring group presented themselves at Hilversum railway station to buy tickets for a sightseeing trip into Amsterdam. Apparently, the sight of such a large and boisterous group flustered the Dutch ticket office clerk to the point that Derek had to take charge - issuing all the tickets himself in the ticket office in true Thomas Cook style. I can also remember getting a 'bollocking' from him in a touring match he was refereeing for 'rough handling' a Dutch player, pointing out this was not setting a good example. He moved to Peterborough when the company's HQ transferred from London. After retirement, he used to assist with various company events such as in-house management conferences, where I met him again many years later on at least one occasion. He was a confirmed bachelor and 'clubman', and when he sadly died in 2001, left a sum of £5,000 in his will to be used for other Thomas Cook retirees, to enjoy a Christmas lunch. Roy Butcher commented that this gift managed to cover their lunches for many years. He embodied the 'spirit' of the rugby section as well as serving in the best tradition of Thomas Cook.

Roy Butcher - learnt his rugby at Brockley Grammar school in South East London, and worked for the civil engineers John Mowlem before joining the company in 1960. He played in the forwards for the first XV and 'A' teams (a white-short non-conformist) and as a member of the Foreign Exchange department knew *The Goat Tavern* well. He was seconded for a tour of duty in Norway which he thoroughly enjoyed, staying in a hotel where his 'ownership' of the odd bottle of Scotch (sourced through NATO contacts) became a useful local currency. He moved to the south coast, based in Dover part of the on-board currency exchange team covering the British Rail ferries to France. He later played for Dover RFC. Now retired, living in Peterborough, is a committee member of Thomas Cook's Benevolent Fund, whilst otherwise enjoying his love of classic motorcycles, owning a couple of AJS machines and a Matchless 600cc which he has taken on tours throughout Europe and no, he's not a *'Hells Angel'* but does have a beard. He is also skilled at repairing vintage Muldivo calculating machines (that's a pre-electronic, foreign currency converter to you and me).

Hugh Dalzell – learnt his rugby as a schoolboy, and one of the stalwarts of the club being Honorary match secretary '61-'65, responsible for the club fixtures as well as being first XV Captain '59-61 and vice Captain 61/2. He was based in Berkeley Street in the Holiday Tours Department (seven-a-sides winners in '58), also played Cricket and Hockey for the company. Described later as *'not just one of the handsome ones in the three-quarter line, but also a diligent match secretary; a hard task master in pre-season training and a creative fly-half responsible for many of our successes'*. This is illustrated by his drop-goal contribution to the club's winning score during the first Hilversum tour in 1958. (My game also improved playing under his encouragement and captaincy). His South London flat in Tooting was the scene of many 'drinkfest' parties for the first XV. He left the company to join the Italian airline Alitalia, playing for Wanstead RFC with Don Keston and later with Mike Lidbetter for Tonbridge RFC for a few seasons. After leaving the airline, he decided to teach and became a lecturer in Travel & Tourism in Surrey. He contributed many photos as well as the once lost Hilversum programme of 1959 for the club's archive. He is now involved with conservation, as

Honorary Secretary of the 'Grand Western Canal Trust' and lives with his wife Jan in Devon.

Robin Garrett – was based at Berkeley Street, in the 5th floor Traffic Management Department. He was once the boxing sparring partner of actor Dennis Waterman's older brother. No doubt this experience helped him 'dodge' the odd tackle playing in the three-quarters and occasionally at full-back. After serving National Service with the RAF at Biggin Hill, he returned to play in the 'A' team during the 1960/3 seasons. A white-short non-conformist, and a pipe-smoker, he was part of the 1963 touring side to Holland. He eventually left the company to join Barclays Bank - he'd been in the team who thrashed them 29-0 at Ravensbourne in 1960. After the rugby section closed, he joined Streatham-Croydon RFC, where he played in the three-quarters, as well as enjoying athletics and speed walking. He is a member of the Thomas Cook Pensioner's Association and a regular attendee at the annual *'Family Gathering'* lunch in Peterborough. Now in his 70's, he recalls Derek Bascombe's kindness at those events as he always went out of his way to give him a lift from the railway station. He's a keen and competitive 'scrabble' player, in addition to the love of travelling which he and his wife continue to enjoy several times a year. He lives in Surbiton, contributed a lost '63/4 fixture list, and believes he still has his old club jersey –somewhere in the garage.

Bobby Gould - he and I (both teenagers at the time) enjoyed a similar sense of humour, which included the decidedly sinister alternative comedian Ivor Cutler. We also made numerous visits to the Spike Milligan *'Running, Jumping & Standing Still'* film showing in Piccadilly in the 1960's we thought it hilarious. He had an older brother (he occasionally played too), who worked in the famous Dobell's Jazz Record shop in Charing Cross Road, a specialist record retailer. It became one of London's best known jazz landmarks. Unfortunately, Bobby received a serious injury during an away match when he was tackled hard into a corner flag, in those days made out of wood. The shaft broke in two and in the tumble, pierced his inner thigh. He was a hospital case, taking him out of the game for the rest of the season. He didn't return to the game, but later left the company and went to work in Smithfield Market as a Bummaree (a self-employed porter -since you may wonder).

Fred Jenkins – was one of the Cook's uniformed staff at Berkeley Street. He'd been in the first tour to Hilversum in 1958 together with his brother Ivor (who had been in a Royal Navy inter-services team against the Army at Twickenham). I didn't know Fred at the time because he'd stopped playing by the time I joined. However, curiously, our paths crossed some thirty years later in the early 1990's. I had joined a Cook's subsidiary responsible for arranging international conferences and incentives, at their newly acquired offices near Buckingham Palace. It was located in a terrace of grand buildings, and had once been used as a hospital for officers during the First World War, run by Sister Agnes a close friend of King Edward VII. Fred was sent from Berkeley Street to help with reception and security duties. (He believed the building was haunted). Hearing his Welsh accent, we would exchange greetings in Welsh like *'bore da'*, and *'nos da'* –good morning/night, and struck up a friendship. During this time Peter Middleton was the company's Chief Executive, (he'd previously been a monk and MI6 officer), who frequently visited the premises when involved with company conference strategy. On his first visit Fred wasn't around so I answered the door. There was, so I thought, a motor-cycle messenger dressed in full black leathers, carrying a helmet. Before I could ask what he was collecting, he'd walked passed and through to the inner offices. Later the same day Fred and I were in reception when another visitor in the form of the lovely Vicki Michelle arrived. She was the actress who played Yvette in the long-running BBC One situation comedy *'Allo Allo'*- a celebrity being hired for a part in the conference programme. She was as gorgeous in the flesh as she appeared on television. One lunch-time whilst browsing a local remaindered bookshop I came across *'Welsh Rugby: the crowning years '68-'80,* and on impulse bought two copies. I gave one to Fred. He responded *'I know him'* pointing to one of the authors Clem Thomas, one time Welsh international and (then) a newspaper columnist. *'We drink at the same club in Wales'.* One good turn deserves another. He later managed to get Clem Thomas to sign my copy, on one of his trips 'back home'. My collectors' item!

Dave Keeling - one of the stalwarts, a stocky, blond haired and good natured player in the 'A' team who was one of our best hookers. He eventually became captain in the 1964/5 season. He worked in the Foreign Exchange department at Notting Hill Gate office. He was married and lived in West Hampstead. He also had an attractive younger sister who would occasionally visit Ravensbourne to watch and support some our matches. He had a passion for wearing 'extremely red' socks. This helped my myopia immeasurably playing at scrum half. He and his family were close friends of Mike Lakin.

Mike Lakin – worked in Conducted Tours Department where Bill Trenfield introduced him to the club. Mike became the 'A' team captain for the 1963/4 and then First team captain for the 1964/5 season. To celebrate his captaincy he invited many players, wives and girl-friends to a 'house party' with his wife Sheila in Kenton, which was a great success –although his neighbours would say different. Unknowingly at the time this was to be the autumn of the club activities and that season we lost all 18 recorded matches. After moving to Holiday Tours he earned the 'unique' distinction of being the only club captain to be banned from playing for the club after a heated disagreement with the departmental manager. He went on to play for *Old Masonians* and *Gaytonians* –but as he says *'it was never the same'*. Another 'white shorts' non-conformist, Mike left the company to join Milbank Tours, and later managed a Mecca Leisure ballroom and nightclub business in South Wales. Where apparently on alternative years visiting French supporters would invariably kick the doors in...*'great fun'* as he dryly commented. In the meantime, he managed to enjoy watching many internationals at the old Cardiff Arms Park and Parc de Princes in Paris. On being contacted about this book said *'of course I remember you ...where did you learn all those terrible rugby songs'!* He lives in Wiltshire and enjoys walking his Labrador dog. He also contributed a 'lost' team photograph to help the project. It featured in the Cook's *Pensioners Association 'Bulletin',* to encourage other ex players to respond. It worked.

Mike Lidbetter – a first XV centre three-quarter based in High Street Kensington and later Fleet Street office. He joined the club early on and after a break for National Service with the Royal Engineers at Suez and Cyprus rejoined the company in 1956. He travelled on the first Hilversum tour in 1958 scoring three tries (the highest scorer). He played against them again on their first visit to Ravensbourne a year later. A member of the company inter-departmental seven-a-side team playing for London Offices, -he also played Hockey and owned a Lambretta scooter. He took over the first XV captaincy from Hugh Dalzell for two seasons 1960-62. Mike and Hugh's partnership in the three-quarters brought many successes. He left to join another travel company Wakefield Fortune which later became Hogg Robinson. He also played at Tonbridge RFC for a few seasons. Another club mate Brian Wright was best man at his wedding and he and his wife Val now live in Hampshire.

Harry Masterton–Smith – joined the company in 1960 and was sent straight to Harrods where Roy Bannister recruited him to the club. In previous years he had played for ASV Cologne and Exeter University. A forward, usually second-row, he played for the first XV, against Hilversum at Ravensbourne in 1961 and in the subsequent 1960-2 seasons, -another 'white-short' non-conformist. After what was to be his last match in December 1962 against *Customs & Excise,* a 0-0 draw at Ravensbourne, we experienced a particularly severe winter. The ground was frozen for much of January and February subsequently many matches cancelled. In the spring of 1963 he departed for an overseas posting to Cairo, to *'calm the natives'* as he humorously put it. In previous years there had been a lot of civil unrest cumulating in the Suez War of 1956. The British had become increasingly unpopular in Egypt, with many British institutions set on fire, including the exclusive Turf club. Shepheards hotel - known to tourists all over the world, was badly damaged as well as the Cook's office. Tourism recovered and years later a few old players caught up with him in Egypt including Gerry Silk and Vic Bulmer –Jones who by chance introduced him to his future wife Anne. They now live in Somerset.

Peter Simmonds – worked in a number of London offices including Berkeley Street, Regent Palace (hotel), Selfridges, and Richmond. He learnt his rugby by being introduced to the game and diligently studying the laws. He then went on, like Perrett-Young before him (from the old *Ludgate Circus Club XV),* to qualify as a London Society Rugby Union referee, covering matches in the Greater London area for around four seasons. He played in the second-row for both the First and 'A' XV's from 1958-1963 seasons, playing against the RC Hilversum visitors in 1959 and 1961. He was an all-round sportsman playing cricket and hockey for the company. He enjoyed the odd skiing educational to Italy with Hugh Dalzell and contributed to the 'story' by remembering old club players like 'Pincher' Martin and Freddie Petts. He lives with his wife in Kingston upon Thames.

Derek Sells – another stalwart playing in the forwards, and a particularly good scrummager. He took over the 'A' XV captaincy from Don Keston for two seasons from 1961 to 1963, becoming vice Captain in the 1964/5 season. He had a dry and wicked sense of humour which I found amusing and he helped foster much of the fun and team spirit during that time. He had a fund of amusing asides, one of which has entered my own lexicon, *'when in doubt –kick it out'*. (It was his advice to inexperienced new players). Like many older players in the team, he had been conscripted for National Service in the RAF somewhere in the Middle East. This experience added to his collection of 'bon mots'. Typically during socialising after the match, (he smoked Senior Service) would occasional accept a filter tip cigarette. Holding it quizzically in his fingers referring to it as a *'Gefilte'* tip, (his amusing pun - Gefilte is a Jewish fish ball dish) much to the amusement, of Geoff Brooks and others. Often after losing to an Old Boy side he would as the evening wore on – drawing on his cigarette reflectively, refer to them as the *Old Bastardians*, with his wry sense of humour. He would often adopt a mock disapproval and comment about the smell of my pipe tobacco - I was experimenting with *Balkan Sobranie* at the time. He would say, the smell reminded him of *'Pasha'* cigarettes –again, to much amusement of some of the older players. I discovered these cigarettes had been made from a pungent Turkish tobacco –smelling much like camel dung, and held in contempt by the smoking community (a hangover from war-time necessity, when Virginia tobacco was scarce). They were manufactured by the old Bristol firm of WD & HO Wills.

Pete Shaw – an affable Yorkshireman from Huddersfield. This is the town where Rugby League was born in 1895 after the 'Northern Clubs' 'break-away' meeting at the George hotel. He was part of the first Easter tour to Holland scoring a try which he also converted. He had become one of the early club members in the mid 1950's, working in the Rates Department in Berkeley Street. Legend has it that he was involved in the 'armchair removal' incident (described later) from LMS's clubhouse in Wembley, typically a white-short non-conformist playing in the three-quarters. He left the company and emigrated to Ontario in Canada where he was involved in the Canadian travel business. He would regularly bring tours to the UK on numerous occasions, maintaining his friendship with Roy Bannister meeting whenever there was an opportunity.

Steve Sutcliffe-Hey - his 'party piece' which usually involved a bet, was to say *'punch me as hard as you like (in the stomach) - and I won't feel it'*. It is difficult to do this cold bloodedly and half-heartedly I'd make no effect. The result usually meant buying him drinks. He'd been a Deck Officer in the Merchant Navy, in the Far East and had returned to the UK sharing a house with his brother in Surrey. There was a sense of 'benign madness' about him and to liven up games he would on receiving the ball at full back, often for no tactical reason kick the ball high up (up and under) shouting *'Garryowen'*, (this kick was named after the Irish *Garryowen Football Club* of Limerick, who popularised this tactic in the 1920's). This was hoping the team would rally and chase, by putting the opposition under pressure competing for the high ball. I used to play the occasional game of lawn tennis with him in the summer months at Ravensbourne –and despite his 'robust girth' he won most games effortlessly. (He'd had lots of practice on a court rigged up on the deck of his ship –out East).

6. The opponents

'Haul them down you Zulu warriors,
Haul them down you Zulu King',
I Kama zimba, zimba zimba,
I karma zimba, zimba zee,'

*–a favourite chant with the First team Vice-Captain Jim Munnick in the
1964/5 season, who had travelled to England from an apartheid
South Africa.*

In 'part three' of the club's short history, the combined
teams managed to play over four hundred matches
against something like a hundred different clubs -
losing more than winning, but then it's not all about
'winning or losing -but *'how we played the game'* as the
poet might have said.

It is quite staggering looking back at the fixture lists, of
the wide range and diversity of clubs we played against
during the 1950's and 1960's. This would be
impossible today, with the RFU league system. They
ranged from the high profile well established clubs like
London Scottish, Rosslyn Park and *Wasps.* Old-Boys
sides from Kent and Surrey schools such as
Beccehamians, Caterhamians, Purleians. Colleges and
Medical schools like *Kingston Technical College, Royal
Free, and Kings College Hospitals.* We had fixtures with
business houses such as *British Petroleum, Decca,
Ford, Harrods'* the Knightsbridge department store and
Lyons teashops and corner-houses. Insurance
companies like *Commercial Union* and *Prudential.* Harry
Masterton-Smith recalls playing against a *Coal Board
XV* – but no records survive. We played against
Government and state institutions ranging from the
BBC, Customs & Excise, to the *Civil Service,* and *Port of
London Authority.* Overseas banks like *Chartered* and
Standard, and others like *Barclays, Westminster* and
National Provincial (now merged into Nat West). *British
European Airways* (BEA), which merged with BOAC to
become British Airways. The regional railway
companies such as *Southern, London Midland Scottish*

and *Great Western Railways*. As well as military teams like HAC *Honourable Artillery Company* and the *US Marines* (who took time off from guarding the American Embassy in Grosvenor Square). In addition the club established a regular overseas tour to Holland playing *RC Hilversum sides, RC t'Gooi,* and other University clubs.

A summary of the clubs played 1953 - 1966

Major rugby clubs
London Irish, London Scottish, Rosslyn Park, Saracens, Wasps

Old Boys
Abbotstonians, Anchorians, Askians, Beccehamians, Caterhamians, Cestrians, Colfeians, Creightonians, Elthamians, Elysians, Esthameians, Hamptonians, Hermits, Isleworthians, Ignatians, Loughton, Masonians, Mitchamians, Purleians, Olavians, Shootershillians

Minor clubs
Brighton, Ealing, Esher, Grasshoppers, Hendon, Merton & Morden, Osterley, Rochester, Ruislip Shirley Wanderers, Sidcup, Streatham, Sudbury Court, Twickenham (Exiles), Wanstead, Westcombe Park, Wimbledon

Colleges & Polytechnics
Battersea College, Borough Polytechnic, Goldsmiths College, Kingston Tech, Northern Poly, College of St Mark & St John, Southall Technical College, Woolwich Poly

Military
Battersea Ironsides (ex. *42nd Royal Tank Regiment Cadets XV*), HAC (*Hon Artillery Company*), HMS President *(London Div. RNR)*, U S Marines (based at their London Embassy*)*, King Edward VII Nautical College

Insurance Companies
Cuaco (Commercial Union Assurance Co.), Ibis (Prudential), Royal Exchange Assurance, Sun Alliance,

Government & Institutions	BBC (*British Broadcasting Corporation*), Civil Service, Customs & Excise, London Fire Brigade, London Transport, PLA (*Port of London Authority*), Vet Lab (Government Central Veterinary Laboratory)
Manufacturing & Business Houses	AEC, AEI (Woolwich), CAV, Decca, Firestone, Ford, GEC, Harrodian, Hoover, Lyons, Meadhurst *(British Petroleum)*, Unilever, Smiths Industries (Clocks), V.C.D (*Vickers*)
Hospital medical and dental schools	King's College Hospital, London Hospital, Royal Dental Hospital, Royal Free, University College Hospital
UK Banks & Foreign Exchange	Bank of England, Barclays, Lloyds, National Provincial Bank, Westminster, Forex (London Foreign Exchange)
Overseas Banks	Chartered Bank of India, Standard Bank of South Africa, Bank of London and South America
Airlines	Silver Wings (BEA-British European Airways), Speedbird (BOAC)
Railways	Great Western Railways (GWR), London Midland Scottish Railway (LMS), Southern Railway
Misc. clubs	Centymca, Fairbain House (Boys Club), Juno, Plebs, Princes Gate, Toch H,
Exiles clubs	London French, London New Zealand
Overseas clubs	(Holland) RC Hilversum, RC t'Gooi, possibly Delft and or Leiden University sides

The 'big name' 19th Century clubs we played

Out of the total fixtures we played, most of our opponents were from Old Boys and Business houses. However, our fixture secretary did secure a number of games against the 'big' established London clubs. At this time there were about nine or so major clubs many of which many became founder members of the Rugby Football Union when it was formed in 1871. We had managed to arrange fixtures with five of them – three of which are now professional, playing in the Premiership, including *London Irish, Wasps* and *Saracens*. The other clubs *London Scottish* and *Rosslyn Park* have remained amateur but both feature within the top thirty clubs in the National English League system. We lost more games than we won, but had our best success against *London Scottish*, winning on two occasions, one of which I played in at their Richmond Athletic Ground. When these clubs were formed they described themselves as Football Clubs – rather than *Rugby* Football clubs, this often distinguishes the older clubs.

London Irish FC *(est.1898)*
Played 1, Lost 1
Famous players*: Tony O'Reilly, (Ireland, Barbarians -33 appearances and British Lions'), Jeremy Davidson, (Ireland, British Lions')*

As the 19th century drew to a close there was a consensus of opinion on both sides of the Irish Sea that a sporting club for Irishmen in London was badly needed. Part of the inspiration for this was the example of the exiles from the other home countries, *London Scottish* had been formed in 1878 and *London Welsh* seven years later in 1895. These clubs offered their countrymen a home away from home in London, a place to meet and relax while employment or education or other reasons took them away from their home country. So it was in 1898 that a group of Irishmen came together to form their own club, the *London Irish Rugby Football Club*. The founding fathers were an exceptional group of powerful personalities embracing politicians, lawyers and businessmen united by a sense of Irishness and passion for rugby. From the beginning London Irish was to provide a welcoming 'home' and hospitable meeting place for all Irish people, regardless of creed or politics. For the *London Irish* the Sixties started in September, 1959 with a suitably 'swinging' festive opening of the new facilities at the ground in Sunbury. This was a great season for them, not losing a game. Over the seasons, their ground has seen good wins but many defeats, with many talented players such Mike Gibson, Tony O'Reilly and Ollie Waldron, who all graced the Sunbury pitch. Our only fixture was played by the First team against their extra 'A's losing at home 5-9 with that close score it's a pity we didn't have a return match. Unfortunately, we were never able to enjoy success or failure in their immortal *Fitz's Bar*, an old wooden shed that once stood at the end of the ground. It originally served as changing rooms and a tea room however it became the place to drink when the new stand opened. The bar was ruled over by *Fitzy* himself who tried to keep a happy, respectable house despite the best efforts of many over the years to compromise the reputation of his unique hostelry. It was torn down in 1975, soon after which Fitz –George Fitzpatrick died. His ashes were scattered where the bar stood.

London Scottish FC *(est.1878)*
Played 6, Won 2, Drawn 1, Lost 3
Famous players: *Gavin Hastings (Scotland, British Lions' - Capt.), Mike Campbell-Lamerton (Army, Scotland, British Lions' as Capt.)*
London Scottish Football Club was founded in April 1878 at MacKay's Tavern, Water Lane, Ludgate Hill, close to the Old Thomas Cook head office in Ludgate Circus. The inaugural meeting determined the playing strip of Blue shirts with a Red Lion, White shorts and Red Socks which still remains the colours of the club more than 130 year later. It is also the oldest

established club, out the three home country 'exiles' in London. With the Earl of Rosebery as the club's first President, they initially played at Blackheath Common. As the club thrived they added some respected opponents like *Oxford* and *Cambridge Universities* and *Harlequins* to the fixture list, moving ground to the Old Deer Park in Richmond as tenants of *Richmond Cricket Club*. Finally in 1894 moving to their present ground the Richmond Athletic Ground which they share with *Richmond Football Club*. Over the years they have an enviable record of producing in the region of over two-hundred Scottish Internationals as well as four British Lions' captains. We were hammered 0-40 in our first game and season encounter in 1953. By the time of the 1959/60 season we fielded both First and 'A' teams against them at Richmond. The First XV won 27-3 and 'A' lost 3-16, which was encouraging. The following season only the 'A' team played losing narrowly 11-12. The final matches were played in the 1961/2 season where the First XV held them to a draw at Ravensbourne whereas the 'A' team away at Richmond had a great victory winning 16-0. We enjoyed some great evenings with them –apart from *The Ball of Kirriemuir* one other amusing verse to a song I recall, sung in a broad Scottish accent, at a brisk pace, in their clubhouse, to the tune of the *'Road to the Isles'*:

'There's a Gentleman's convenience down the steps at Waterloo,
There's another for the ladies further on,
For a penny on deposit you can hire a water closet,
Season tickets are only half-a-crown.'

(Rugger enthusiasts will know, Waterloo is the departure station for Twickenham, a penny, about 2.4p and half-a-crown is 12.5p in new money)

Another (and this sounds like a successful family business model) was the amusing *'My God How the Money Rolls In'*, sung to the tune of *'Bring Back My Bonnie'*

My father makes book on the corner,
My mother makes illicit gin,
My sister sells kisses to sailors,
My God how the money rolls in.'

CHORUS:
'Rolls in, rolls in,
My God how the money rolls in, rolls in,
Rolls in, rolls in,
My God how the money rolls in.

After the game turned professional, the club had a successful start to the new era playing in the Premiership, however unfortunately at the end of the 1998/9 season the club was forced into administration. The original amateur club then rejoined the leagues but was effectively demoted 9 leagues by the RFU. Subsequently the club has gained six promotions in nine years and now plays in National League 1.

Rosslyn Park FC *(est. 1879)*
Played 1, Lost 1
Famous players: *Prince Alexander Obolensky (England), Paul Ackford (England, British Lions')*
One of the old established clubs founded in 1879 when a group of young cricketers decided to form a football club (as rugby clubs were often called then) in order to stay together during the winter months. They had originally played cricket in the grounds of Rosslyn House, part of the Rosslyn Park Estate and had adopted the name 'Rosslyn Park'. It continued with the formation of a rugby club. In their first season they played on a ground near Hampstead Heath Station and hired a room in the White Horse pub as a changing room, and a place to store their goal posts. In 1892, Baron Pierre de Coubertin was instrumental in bringing the club to Paris. They became the first English club to play rugby in Europe when they played *Stade Francais* in Paris. In 1894 they moved to the Old Deer Park, Richmond, which they shared with *Old*

Merchant Taylors until moving to Roehampton in 1956. The same year we played them at home losing narrowly 6-8. In the 1930's they had the legendary Prince Obolensky playing for them who also played for England helping to secure their first win against the *All Blacks*. Since 1939 *Rosslyn Park* has organised and run the *Schools Sevens Tournament*, starting with 16 schools, and by 1996, 350 schools were taking part. It is the world's largest Sevens Tournament. We played just one game against them in 1956 after the original *Foreign Office* fixture was cried off. Today, playing in National 1 league they still rank amongst the top thirty clubs in the country and have over 800 playing members.

Saracens FC *(est.1876)*
Played 4, Won 1, Lost 1, Cancelled/unrecorded 2
Famous Players: *Jason Leonard (England, British Lions'), Francois Pienaar, (South Africa - Captain at the famous 'Mandela Final' victory in the 1995 World Cup)*

In 1876 the *Saracens Football Club* was founded by the Old Boys of the Philological School in Marylebone (later to become Marylebone Grammar School) and its first fixture was at Primrose Hill playing fields with the *'red star and crescent'* worn. They amalgamated with a neighbouring club, the *Crusaders*, in 1878. By the 1950/1 season they celebrated their 75th anniversary, and the overall membership increased to over seven hundred with 110 playing members. In the 1960's one of their ex skippers' V.J. Harding was awarded a third blue at Cambridge, and became subsequently the second International Saracen, playing for England (1961-2). Our first encounter in 1955 at home was lost decisively 0-17. A subsequent fixtures in 1957 was won 23-17, later matches were cancelled or unrecorded.

Wasps RUFC *(est.1867)*
Played 1, Lost 1
Famous players: Rob Andrews (England, British Lions'), Gareth Rees (Canada), Lawrence Dellaglio (England, British Lions'), Roger Uttley (England, British Lions')

Our one and only game against this side was in 1955 losing at home narrowly 14-17, and needless to say not one of the above were able to play against us (on account of being too young or yet un-born). *Wasps RUFC* was originally formed in 1867 at the now defunct Eton and Middlesex Tavern in North London, before the advent of the Rugby Football Union as an administrative body. The Club gained its name largely due to the fashion of the Victorian period when clubs tended to adopt the names of insects, birds and animals. The name in itself has no particular significance other than this vogue. Wasps were invited to join the Union and, therefore, were eligible to be Founder Members. And so they would have been had it not been for a calamitous mix-up that led to them not being present at the inauguration ceremony. In true rugby fashion the team turned up at the wrong pub, on the wrong day, at the wrong time and so forfeited their right to be called Founder Members. The Club's first home was in Finchley Road, North London, eventually they moved to their home in Sudbury, buying the ground outright. Although the team currently play at the *Adams Park Stadium,* High Wycombe, on home match-days, the Sudbury clubhouse still exists and Sudbury is still considered the Club's spiritual home by diehard fans.

From banks to railways and buses to teashops - Some other club opponent sketches

From business houses, banks, and insurance companies, to college old boys, military units, institutions, exiles, railways and airlines - we played against them! These Saturday afternoon amateur players, in their day jobs - made red London buses, protected the realm, handled our insurance, looked after us if we were sick or had tooth-ache, informed and entertained us on the radio, provided rail and air travel services, offered us banking and cheque book facilities, and provided premises to enjoy a nice cup of tea, and a cup-cake!

AEC (The Associated Equipment Company) RFC
Played 5: Won 2, Drawn 1, Lost 2
The game results against this club were about even, except for one big loss in particular. *AEC* had their ground in Southall, and were the builders of the famous London red buses from 1912 to 1979. The company merged with British Leyland in 1962, and eventually production closed in 1979. In one memorable game (but for the wrong reason) in March 1961 towards the end of season at an 'A' team away fixture, we could only field 14 players. *AEC* kindly offered to lend us a player, who in fact turned out to be better than anyone in our team. To rub it in, as the game developed their captain even agreed with our skipper (Don Keston) that they would not subsequently convert any of their tries, *'to make a game if it'!* This was a humiliating defeat. They scored thirteen tries (three points each) and had converted the first (another two points) making it a 0-41 defeat (the largest recorded). There were some players in the 'A' XV that actually didn't know there were fifteen players in a team, as quite often we'd be playing one man short. This was humorously characterised in Michael Green's book *'The Art of Course Rugby'*, published a year earlier. After the *AEC* business operation closed many of their rugby players joined the *GWR club*.

Battersea Ironsides RFC
Played 10: Won 1, Lost 4, Drawn 1,
Cancelled/unrecorded 4
In the early matches against this club they were wanderers – today they have a home ground in Earlsfield South London. The club originally known as

42nd Royal Tank Regiment Cadets XV, founded in 1943 by Colonel E H St Maur Toope from members of the Regiment's Cadet Battalion located in the Borough of Battersea. It was an armoured regiment of the British Army, part of the Royal Armoured Corps. Their motto *'Through the mud and the blood to the green fields beyond'* is reflected in the regimental colours Brown, Red and Green. A year later the regiment took part in the invasion of Normandy in 1944; after the war, in 1948 the club name was changed to *'Battersea Ironsides'*. 'Ironside' being the affectionate name for the World War Two Armoured Tank, and the club was opened up to players other than ex-Royal Tank Regiment Cadets. As their Colonel wrote in his memoirs *"...I was successful in lifting the ban on intoxicating liquor served to cadets in the Home Guard Canteen at Clapham Junction Drill hall, to which most of the team returned, and thus the boys were introduced to the other reason for playing Rugger – a pint or two of the best!"*. Today Battersea Ironsides describes themselves as a small, friendly social rugby club, renowned for its hard rugby, located just seven miles from the centre of London. This is the club where I learnt the lyrics to a popular war-time army song –sung to the tune of *'The Colonel Bogey March'*,

> *'Hitler, has only got one ball,*
> *Göring, has two but very small,*
> *Himmler, is somewhat sim'lar,*
> *But poor Goebbels has no balls at all'.*

I recall being involved in a heated brawl during an 'A' XV match at the beginning of the 1962 season, (which we narrowly lost 12-13) the referee blew his whistle. Taking me aside and said *'do you know rule 79?'* I replied *'err, not off hand Sir'* (referees were always Sir). *'Well, it's un-gentlemanly conduct on the rugby pitch'*. It was my warning about behaviour. Sin bins hadn't been invented. I discussed this with one of their players in the bar afterwards –and the response was *'oh he's (the referee) Army type - always quoting that'* There is no such rugby union rule –or law. He was apparently referring to Article 79 in the 'Articles of War' concerning *'Disgraceful Conduct...unbecoming the character of an officer and gentleman',* but the lesson had been learnt. Today they play in RFU London & S.E. region – Surrey league 2.

BBC RFC
Played 4: Won 3 Lost 1
The *British Broadcasting Corporation* had an absolutely magnificent ground at Motspur Park near Barnes Station in South West London.

The walk towards its gates through the drive way, leading off the Motspur Road was like arriving at an exclusive 'home counties' country club. The white painted double-story club house building was in the colonial 'pavilion' style complete with clock tower. The extensive grounds included four football pitches, six tennis courts, one hockey pitch, one rugby pitch, two cricket squares, and a rifle range –no less! In my first season with the 'A' team in October 1959, we won 14-0 and more importantly I scored my 'first try' in club rugby, playing at centre. Adjacent to the changing areas it had a splendid array of bath-tubs lined up in a row for the after game soak. Luxury! Following the decline in the Corporation's sports activities, it had become disused, so the BBC sold its ground in 2005 to an Irish millionaire developer for £3 million. However local opposition to the proposed scheme was strong, and the latest plans are suggesting that the sports ground could be turned into a cemetery (how ironic). This is because planning regulations required the land to remain as a green space and a cemetery is one of the very few options now open to the owners.

Brighton FC *(est.1868)*
Played 2: Won 1, Lost 1
Now known as the 'Brighton Blues' this club, with their original administration headquarters in *Waters Wine Bar* at the bottom of Spring Street, where committee meetings were held over a dock glass of Sherry was established in 1868. This away fixture was about as far as we travelled, but it did have the allure of the seaside! In September 1962 I was invited to join the First XV for the season's first fixture which we duly won 30-0 (largest recorded), at their (then) ground in the Withdean Stadium (currently being used by *Brighton & Hove Albion FC*, with a capacity of 9,000). This made the win all the more satisfying as mostly we played on park playing fields. After the game we moved to the Castle Square area close to the sea front and the famous pier to enjoy a pint or two. The rugby pub then was in Steine Lane at the rear of the *Royal Pavilion Tavern* known as *Shades Bar*. It was a small busy and noisy bar –and just right for us. This is where I learnt the Roedean School Song, (a local public girls boarding school on the cliffs outside Brighton), needless to say the imagined performances of these strapping girls, are legendary, the opening line - sung to the tune of 'We shall overcome' declares, *'We are from Roedean, good girls are we'* – although the following verses beg to differ, as does the ending chorus, *'Up school, up school, up school, Right up school'!* The pub was (it no longer exists) located in an historic building dated from the late eighteenth century and one of the previous owners had put up a sign referring to it as a 'Gin Palace'. Apparently, Mrs Fitzherbert, (the first wife of the Prince Regent) who resided opposite in Steine House, objected to this and so the word 'shades' was used, it subsequently became a local word for a bar. Whether it was used because it was in the shade of Steine House or because of the shady nature of the business is not clear! The late summer weekend drew on and most of the team returned to London. Some stragglers including myself, Derek Sells, Bobbie Gould, I think

Pete Davies too, decided to stay on. Much later, after a fish & chip supper, (which always tastes better at the seaside), we wandered along to the *Belgrave Hotel* (now Una hotels and totally refurbished), situated on the corner of West Street and Kings Road on the seafront, to seek a room for the night. This hotel was then, in a pretty decrepit state, (think – the *Villa Bella* the hotel featured in the *'Jolly boys Outing'* episode' of BBC TV's *'Only Fools and Horses'*). We negotiated a cheap large room in the garret for us all to sleep in. This weekend cost several weeks' spending money (no credit cards then) which was why a number of us took extra evening jobs to help fund this lavish life-style. Today the *Brighton Blues* play in RFU London 2 SE league.

Chartered Bank of India RFC
Played 16: Won 5, Drawn 2, Lost 5, Cancelled/unrecorded 4

We played against this bank more than most clubs. It merged with Standard Bank in 1969 forming the Standard Chartered Group. Chartered bank was a strong fixture –and only the 'First' team played against them. Chartered sports ground was in East Moseley. From 1955 to 1964 we lost the first four encounters and had to wait until 1962 for our first win, 5-0 away at East Moseley. The Chartered Bank of India, Australia and China (to give its full title) had been founded in 1853 following a grant of a Royal Charter by Queen Victoria. The bank opened its first branch in Bombay with others in Calcutta and Shanghai, followed by Hong Kong and Singapore in 1859. Traditional trade was in cotton from Bombay, indigo and tea from Calcutta, rice from Burma, sugar from Java, tobacco from Sumatra, hemp from Manila and silk from Yokohama. Playing a major role in the development of trade with the East particularly after the Suez Canal opened in 1869. It was once a large country estate and house known as the 'Wilderness'. It was demolished and the park developed as a high-class residential estate in 1876. The site was occupied by

East Molesey Court, a red brick house, built about 1880 in Jacobean style. In 1929 the house, together with the land on the other side of the Mole, was laid out as a sports ground, firstly for the Distillers Company, and then for the Trollope and Colls Group. The estate then became the sports ground of the Standard Chartered Bank. A disastrous fire gutted the house in 1983. The ground was sold and their rugby club closed. The banking group seems to have no official archivist and nowadays devotes a considerable effort into general sports sponsorship –notably *Liverpool FC*.

CUACO (Commercial Union Assurance Co.) RFC
Played 12: Won 2, Drawn 2, Lost 6, Unrecorded 2

The *Cuaco rugby club* was established in 1926, for the employees of Commercial Union Assurance Company, which had been incorporated in 1885. Both the First and 'A' teams played this club many times loosing more than winning. The company ground and sports pavilion was in Lee Green, Kent. Local records show they expanded the clubs bar in 1960 with a building extension, no doubt encouraged by, and to celebrate a win over Cook's in January, as the 'A' team lost away 3-22. Overall we enjoyed a friendly camaraderie with them playing over ten games during fours seasons 1960- 1964. However, 1963 was not a good year for *Cuaco* as we beat them 25-0 in March at our home ground in Ravensbourne, then in the August the company sustained a staggering (then) loss of £1m due to the 'Great Train Robbery (Ronnie Biggs et al) on the Glasgow to Euston mail train. Two year later the rugby club closed (the same year as Cooks). As the Aviva archivist Anna Stone, said *'their rugby club administrators ongoing moan in the company 'house magazine' was the lack of playing members, at one time this was even expressed in verse'*. Their Cricket Club however was more established and survives today. It had purchased a separate ground at Elm Lane, Catford, before moving to Beckenham in 1970. The club remained there until midway through the 2001 season, when its ground was sold to *Crystal Palace FC* for £1m. This was as a result of the take-over of Commercial Union by Norwich Union (now Aviva). The new company was unwilling to underwrite company sporting activities. The cricket club merged with Old Dunstonians CC. Today, Aviva is the new sponsor of the Rugby Premiership in the 2010/11 season.

Fairbairn House
Played 1: Drawn 1
This was a London East End Boy's Club in Canning Town, which had many sports teams –but was best known for its boxing. Most clubs we played were social and friendly. Of course there was rivalry and we played hard – but they were sporting. The first fixture against this club was a disaster. Playing at Ravensbourne on New Year's Eve 1960, became such a brawl it effectively was abandoned as a 0-0 draw. Their team had, it would appear been drawn from their boxing members. The club had been created around 1900 through the Oxford Mansfield settlement idea, to help under privileged East-Enders. No-doubt they thought the Victorian values of the game would rub-off on the club. However, their players took a different view. What should have been a social and friendly game quickly became little more than a free-for-all - a riotous assembly between two sides. We cancelled the following season's fixture.

Great Western Railway – GWR FC
Played 3: Won 1, Lost 2
Cook's RFC played only three games against this old established railway club in the Season 1955-6 – winning one and losing two. Their 17 acre ground was located at Castle Bar Park, Ealing, in West London. *The Great Western Railway Football Club* was formed shortly after the First World War, part of a wider and older Athletic Sports Club. The club's history refers to the season of 1955/6 as their 'golden period'. It was

only Cook's second season, so the win 9-3 was particularly creditable in the first away match. Later in the same season we lost the return match at home by a narrow margin 3-6. Their history records that they 'purloined' the BBC's house flag from Motspur Park. The GWR being a railway side (their routes extended to South Wales and the West Country) found themselves with a seemingly endless supply of expatriate Welshmen - rail locomen and local schoolmasters, playing for them. Today they play in RFU Herts. & Middx. Merit tables.

The HAC Rugby Club *(est.1896)*
Played 1: Won 1
The Cook's 'A' team played this club, as a result of a changed fixture because *Royal Free Hospital* cried-off. We played in December 1959, winning 18 -13 against a full Army side. The Honourable Artillery Company has a superb historical home ground in the heart of the City of London. It's well hidden behind buildings of Bunhill Row, Chiswell Street and City Road, where its 'castle like gateway' entrance is located. I do remember one of their songs which was sung to the tune of *'The British Grenadiers'* which is their regimental quick march, (a popular song from the 18th century, featured in Tom Brown's schooldays, -although no doubt sung to the original words).

> *'We like the girl's who say they will,*
> *We like those girl's who don't,*
> *We don't like those who say they will*
> *-but then they say they won't.*
> *But of all the girls we like the best,*
> *We may be wrong or right,*
> *Are the girl's who say they never will?*
> *- but look as though they might!*

The regiment is the oldest in the British Army and the second most senior unit of the Territorial Army, established in the reign of Henry VIII in 1537. It has been at its present site since 1641. During the time of the Great Plague it was used as a burial site in 1665. The ground was the location of the first ever hot air balloon ascent in England (by Vincenzo Lunardi) in 1784 in front of huge crowds. The courtesy prefix 'Honourable' was officially confirmed by Queen Victoria in 1860. When we played this club they comprised solely of members from the Regiment. However, by the early 1970s like many other closed clubs it opened its membership to Non-Regimental players. Today, they play in Herts & Middx. league 2. The ground is also used for corporate hospitality, and local schools can use the ground for sporting activity, but the grounds remain at the disposal of the Regiment for training purposes.

Harrodian RFC
Played 1: Lost 1
The first team had only one fixture with this club in 1962 losing away 3-29. The club was established in the 1920's, with their clubhouse in Lonsdale Road Barnes. Originally the ground was the recreational centre for the employees of Harrods Store in Knightsbridge. It had a sports ground, swimming pool, croquet and bowling lawn. *'Unfortunately, the flaw in this strategy* as Michael Whitfield, Chairman of *Barnes RFC*, the successor of the original club, commented *'was their employees have to work Saturdays!'*, so needless to say it became an open club. This famous store, established in 1834 by Charles Henry Harrod a tea merchant, moved to its present Knightsbridge site in 1849, to take advantage of the trade generated by the Great Exhibition of 1851 (As did Thomas Cook) in nearby Hyde Park. In 1988 the store's Egyptian owner Mohamed Al-Fayed sold the 25 acre ground to a new independent day school which opened in 1993 as The Harrodian School. A year later the *Harrodians RFC* moved to its present ground in Barn Elms, and became absorbed into *Barnes RFC*, but still has some Harrods staff playing. The Sunday and touring side is known as

Sinners RFC, formed in 1966. Today they play in RFU National league 3 London SE.

IBIS -Prudential Assurance Co. RFC
Played 10: Won 3, Lost 5, Unrecorded 2

Their rugby club founded in 1933 was part of Prudential's Ibis Society, established for the benefit of its employees. Its full title was The Prudential Clerks' Society. It comprised a number of clubs, such as a literary club, a Christian fellowship, a shooting club, and a number of sports teams including rugby. As Morgannis Graham, Prudential archivist explained *'The name Ibis was supposedly derived from the shouts of 'Come on I-Bees!' at sports games, as the Industrial Branch (IB) of the company was apparently more popular than the Ordinary Branch (OB)'*. They had a thirty acre sports ground close to the river Thames in Chiswick, with a pre-war art deco style pavilion. These playing field were shared with others clubs like *St Thomas's Hospital*. The first match in 1959 was played by the 'first' team losing heavily away 0-32; however the 'A' team made amends being the only Cook's side to win 16-12 at the Chiswick ground in 1962. The company usually known as the Pru, - was established as the Prudential Mutual Assurance and Loan Association in 1848, and today is an international retail financial services company with significant operations in Asia, the US and the UK. In 1965 they moved 1,700 staff into Forbury House, the new Prudential building at Reading. The rugby club seems to have faded away around 1972 and the Chiswick sports ground closed in 1991. The Ibis name continues, with sports facilities at their grounds in Craigforth, near Stirling Scotland (with a rugby club) and Tilhurst near Reading, alas without one.

Kings College Hospital FC *(Est. 1869)*
Played 1: Lost 1

We only managed one game against this old established and strong hospital side in October 1960, when the 'A' team played their Ex. B side at Ravensbourne narrowly losing 5-6. This club had been established in 1869, one of the oldest in the world, when a group of members formed a rugby club representing faculties including the Medical Department. This was many years before the Rugby Football Union came into being. By that time the London hospitals had established the Inter-Hospital Challenge Cup, played every season from 1874. Like many clubs their fortunes ebbed and flowed as they record on one occasion '...*the difficulty in raising teams is overwhelming. Richmond Club claims our heavy forwards and our best half, hospital duties seem to claim others, whilst general slackness and old age appear to render others a suitable excuse for not playing'*. The inter-war years provided them with a number of celebrity players including an England and British Lions' captain, as well as Scottish and Irish Internationals. The period during which Cook's played, in the 1950's and 1960's, was a difficult time for them. For example in 1955 their entire 1st XV and 'A' XV were due to qualify and complete their medical training, stripping the teams of their vital playing asset. They had barely recovered by 1960 and despite winning against us, lost 15 out of 22 matches played that year. I played in the match at Ravensbourne and recall an incident. On the same Saturday members of the Cook's association football team were also playing. As usual a light hearted sports rivalry and banter would take place on the merits of each game. In the bar afterwards one nameless soccer player, started by sneering at our kit remarking, – '*still wearing 'milk-jug' boots I see*, (a reference to our unfashionable boot design), followed by '*real men' play with round balls'*. Before the usual expletive reply, one of our opponents, an erudite Irish medical student responded for us all, giving him the benefit of his medical knowledge, '*now listen, the shape of real men's balls are actually oval – feel your own balls and tell me if they are not oval- surely any young man will find out it's true'*. With hands in our pockets, and loud cheers, we drank to that! King's was still managing to field five teams and in 1965 won a 'Hospital's Cup' match for the first time in seven seasons. Their famous clubhouse on Dog Kennel Hill built in 1921 was burnt down in 1975. It was re-built, but the inevitable redevelopment found a Sainsbury's Superstore supplanted on their ground. They now play their homes games at the Griffin Sports Club at Dulwich Village. They are an open club and play in RFU London & S.E. region – Kent league 2.

London Midland Scottish Railway -LMS RFC
Played 8: Won 3, Cancelled/unrecorded 5

Cook's had a long established business relationship with LMS railway, and had been partners in the building of Prestatyn holiday camp in North Wales known as *'The Chalet Village by the Sea'* which opened in 1939 (just in time to be requisitioned as an Army barracks during WW2). The club was established in 1927 and their ground in Wembley was the scene of some of the club's largest victories between 1959 -64. No doubt to celebrate one of these, Roy Bannister recalls that the entrance to their clubhouse bar was through an anti-room which has a collection of various sofa's and armchairs. Two nameless players (although one is thought to be Pete Shaw) from the Cook's XV enquired 'innocently' if one of these armchairs 'was free' - seeing it unoccupied the opposition response was 'yes'. Taking them at their word –the two lifted the armchair and carried it to the underground station, eventually depositing it at the left luggage office at Victoria railway station. The following week it was transported to Ravensbourne where it stayed as a 'rugby' trophy'. Like many 'house' clubs recruitment was becoming difficult and it became an open club, but closed at the season's end in 1966 – as did Cook's RFC.

London French RFC
Played 3: Won 1, Lost 1, Cancelled 2
The exile team London French was formed in 1959 on October 21st (ironically this is also Trafalgar Day)! They no doubt enthusiastically declared, *'Allons enfants de la Patrie, Le jour de gloire est arrivé'*- the opening lines of *'La Marseillaise.* A group of older stagiaires (Old Boys) from the French Lycée in London decided that the unadventurous style of English rugby was not to their liking - they wanted to play 'Champagne Rugby' (didn't we all). Our first game in March 1962 was at Ravensbourne, (they were initially a nomadic side), which we won 3-0. For the first four or five seasons they generally played Sunday Rugby only, as many of their members also played for other clubs on a Saturday as well. In 1964 they changed to playing fixtures on a Saturday –we were one of their first Saturday games, again playing at Ravensbourne, but this time losing 0-11. At this time they had finally established a home ground at Raynes Park. They however still retained a Sunday side called the *'SuperCoqs'* (no comment). In 1980 they re-established links with The French Lycée using their grounds at The King George Memorial Playing Fields. The club has never had a clubhouse preferring the use of quality restaurants (how delightfully continental) and pubs to enhance the fun atmosphere of their social activities. Since the 1970's they have been an open club attracting a cosmopolitan blend of French and other rugby playing nations. They are a particularly social side, and like Cook's before them they've also made tours to Holland. Today their current ground is at Barnes in South West London and they play in RFU Herts. & Middx. league 2.

London New Zealand RFC
Played 2: Won 1, Lost 1
This exiles club was originally established in 1926 with Colonel (later Lord) Freyburg as Chairman. However, the Depression and World War two intervened and the

club was re-established in the 1960's moving to Aorangi Park (Aorangi is Maori for 'Cloud in the sky') in Wimbledon where it leased twelve acres from the All England Tennis club until 1981. It was a home ground where its members could play rugby in pleasant surroundings, and return the hospitality they had enjoyed from so many English clubs and provide a place where young Kiwis could get to know Englishmen in a friendly environment. The First team played them at home in 1965 losing 6-16. Unfortunately for us we were to miss the mid to late 1970's (Cook's club closed in 1966). This apparently was the real heyday of the club, as they knew how to party, and typically, their social functions, like BBQ's and Disco's would have hundred's flocking towards their clubhouse - even the 1978 touring All Blacks made a visit. We all know of the '*Haka*' - a war dance which is chanted (yelled) by the New Zealand *All Blacks* at their opponents before each match. Traditionally it was chanted by Maori warriors before charging into battle. The opening chant is typically: 'Ka mate, Ka Mate, Ka ora, Ka ora, Ka mate, Ka mate, Ka ora, Ka ora' *(It is Death - It is Life - It is Death - It is Life)*. Yes, like the Welsh, rugby to New Zealanders is something of a life or death religion. Today they play in RFU London 2 NW league.

Lyons RFC
Played 8: Won 2, Lost 1, Drawn 1, Cancelled/unrecorded 4

Lyons RFC had its ground at Sudbury Hill in North London. Both the First (14-9) and 'A' XV's (15-13) managed away wins at this ground. They were the 'house' team of the famous catering company J. Lyons & Co Ltd. Many of us can probably remember as children being taken to tea in one of their many teashops. The first one opened in 1894 in Piccadilly, the forerunner of a chain of white and gold fronted teashops which occupied prominent positions in many of London's high streets and suburban towns and cities. In the thirties they built the famous Trocadero

Restaurant near Piccadilly Circus and then built the Corner Houses, huge restaurants with their 'Nippy' waitresses, on four or five floors where orchestras played continuously. In their heyday they undertook Buckingham Palace Garden Parties, catering events at Windsor Castle, London's Lord Mayor's banquets at the Guildhall, Chelsea Flower shows, Wimbledon Lawn Tennis Championships and many more. After the war they built and operated the world's first business computer which they called LEO (Lyons Electronic Office). However the company was beginning to run into financial difficulties and in 1968 the Company sold the ground and *Lyons RFC* had to look for a new premises and a name. The Club found a home at Osterley, and were renamed *Centaurs RFC* becoming an open club. However, despite their best efforts the new club was eventually unable to field regular playing sides, so today *Centaurs* plays only social rugby. The company was finally taken over by Allied Breweries and lost its independence.

Old Beccehamian RFC
Played 6: Won 2, Lost 3, Unrecorded 1
Both the First and 'A' teams played against this club, and by and large over the seasons from 1959 to 1964 results were about even. (*This club is not to be confused with Beckenham RFC established much earlier in 1894, whose post war teams had celebrities players like the actor James Robertson-Justice, who appeared in the famous 'Doctor' films, Maurice Denham, a character actor who played alongside Harrison Ford in 'Raiders of the Lost Ark' and Johnny Craddock who, with wife Fanny formed TV's first celebrity chef pairing. In 1957 the club toured Holland and France apparently in a chartered Brixham trawler*). However I digress, the Old Beccehamians had been formed in 1933 by former pupils of Beckenham County School for boys (later Beckenham and Penge Grammar School for Boys and now Langley Park Boys School). In common with all 'Old Boys' clubs membership was originally restricted

to former pupils of the school and they had several teams playing until the Second World War. After the war the club expanded and began to field more teams, playing most of the home games at Langley Park school in Beckenham (although our away games were played in Hayes). In the early 1960's they relaxed their rules and became an open club. However they did have the drawback of not having a permanent clubhouse and bar. Away games for us meant meeting up in local pubs with the West Wickham Home Guard Club becoming the place for after game entertainment on a Saturday evening. Around the same time they had obtained some financial support from Middlesex County and the RFU to build their first clubhouse and bar in West Wickham. Playing games down the hill at Sparrow's Den where the changing rooms were shared with two soccer teams and often by the newly formed *Shirley Wanderers* (the 'A' team played them once in 1960 losing 5-22 at Home). After matches, we would have a steep climb up Corkscrew Hill to get to their clubhouse. Mike Lakin recalls in one match a visiting cousin of Dave Dowling, a useful player from *Old Cryptians* (Gloucester) helped us to an inspiring win. Today, the club is known simply as Beccehamian RFC, and they play in RFU Kent 1 league.

Old Caterhamians RFC
Played 10: Won 3, Lost 2, Cancelled/unrecorded 5
The Club was founded at a meeting of Old Caterhamians at the Bonnington Hotel, London in 1928, with their very first match against *Southern Railways* (a regular Cook's fixture). After the war, the Club became open and for a time used the Dene Field next to St Mary's Church. During the 1950's the club was fielding a number of teams which continued until the early seventies. Their first Clubhouse (reclaimed from a golf course) was erected in 1958 adjacent to the pitch. Both First and 'A' teams played against them between 1956 and 1964 -3 were cancelled, but the 'A' side managed a spectacular win 56-0 (biggest margin

ever) at their ground in 1961. By 1965 they had extended the building by buying an ex-army barrack hut from Aldershot for £50. Their clubhouse was rebuilt in the 1990's and today they have a thriving club which include junior, mini and a Women's XV, their ground is at Park Avenue, Caterham Surrey. They play in RFU Surrey league 2.

Old Ignatians RFC
Played 2: Lost 2

Only the 'A' team played this catholic college, twice, in the 1960/1 season losing at home and losing again the following season at their ground 3-35. As an opposition they had a real sense of purpose and played hard (Jesuit training?), as I can recall playing against them in Tottenham. The Old Ignatians RFC was founded in 1949 to provide rugby for former pupils of St. Ignatius College originally founded 1894. The match we played was on their College pitches in Park Lane, Tottenham. The college's motto and that of its religious community is *'Ad majorem Dei gloriam'* so known by the abbreviation AMDG, the motto of the Society of Jesus, commonly referred to as 'the Jesuits'. The society is a religious order within the auspices of the Roman Catholic Church. The Latin motto means *'For the greater glory of God'* and is believed to have been coined by the founder of the religious order, Saint Ignatius of Loyola, as a cornerstone of the society's philosophy. During the match in 1961, (we had one of their Jesuit priests as referee) there would be many appeals for *'forgive me father'* instinctive responses from their players, repeated to any transgressions of the laws of the game – as adjudicated by the priest's whistle. We finally lost heavily to this onslaught 3-35 (seven converted tries to one unconverted try). They had no clubhouse – as it was a school playing field, so afterwards we adjourned to a local pub the *Bell & Hare* in the High Road, (a popular haunt of Tottenham Hotspur fans because their ground 'White Hart Lane' was nearby). During the socialising, we learnt that most of the Old Ignatians we played against, still recalled the special form of corporal punishment administered at the school. The priests never used a cane, instead it was the ferula (whale bone covered in leather) which was administered on one hand. In serious cases the punishment would be twice six on two hands, but administered on separate days on account of the hand becoming numb, -shades of the inquisition? Corporal punishment ended in the early 1990s. (They had it hard in 'them days', not like the namby-pambies of today who might be given detention instead). Later that evening, on the night bus back to the West End I was sitting on the top deck laughing and chatting away with Bobbie Gould – when suddenly out of the blue a punch landed on the back of my head, momentarily stunned, I turned to see the perpetrator –a short hefty woman, disappearing down the bus stairs who shouted back at my quizzical face – *'that's cos you speak posh'*... and as an after though, *'cos you play rugby'*. (Think Mo Harris the 'mouthy' market trader in BBC TV's *EastEnders*). The college remained at Stamford Hill as a grammar school until 1968, when it became comprehensive. The rugby club moved to South Woodford in 1961 –but by the 1970's the new M11 motorway expansion had purchased the land, so they moved again to Enfield. During the 1980's the club became open and merged with Enfield Old Grammarians. Today they are known as Enfield Ignatians RFC and play in RFU London 2 NE league.

Royal Free Hospital RFC *(est. 1867)*
Played 1: Lost 1, Cancelled 1

Like the other London teaching hospitals they began playing rugby union in the 1860s, with many of its members' former Cambridge and Oxford graduates. The United Hospitals Rugby Football Club was formed in 1867, before the founding of the Rugby Football Union, and by 1874 had initiated the *United Hospital's Challenge Cup*, a competition for the rival hospitals. The First team played this club away in 1959, loosing narrowly 3-6. Later in 1998 University College (one our first games and largest loss, 0-66), Middlesex School of Medicine merged with the Royal Free Hospital Medical School to form the Royal Free and University College Medical School. In 2008 the medical school changed its name to UCL Medical School and a year later to The Royal Free, University College and Middlesex Medical Students (forming the acronym known as the RUMS).

Sidcup RFC *(Est. 1883)*
Played 8: Won 1, lost 6, Unrecorded 1
Sidcup is one of the old Kent sides established in late 19th century. They were a strong fixture for us, playing them seven times between 1955 and 1962 the 'A' team lost both matches (by big margins), and the 'First' only managed one win in 1960. As with most amateur clubs they experienced fluctuating fortunes over the years, but they can boast some players who became internationals, like Jim Staples who captained Ireland, William Pratten of Scotland, Billy Bushell and Andy Hancock of England (whose legendary try – at Twickenham in 1965 drew the Calcutta Cup Match). Today they field some 16 teams from minis through juniors and colts to the four senior Saturday XVs; and play in RFU London 1 North league.

Silver Wings RFC (British European Airways -BEA)
Played 12: Won 3, Lost 7, Unrecorded 2
We won our first two (recorded) fixtures in the 1960/1 season – the First team away at Northolt won 8-6 and the same day the 'A' team won at home 6-0. It went down hill from then on. Cook's had a long established business relationship with BEA. Both companies later teamed up in 1968 (they were facing losses because of stiff competition from charter flights) to promote 'Silver Wing' package holidays in a determined attempt to capture a bigger share of the mass market. *British Airways Rugby Football Club* (as it is today) was originally two clubs the airlines BEA and BOAC (the 'A' XV played them once in 1963 loosing 3-9), established

in the 1950's. They had initially joined forces in 1954 – but soon broke away only to eventually merge again in the 1976/7 season. In the early 1950's BEA were playing against teams like *Met Police, Harlequins* and *Richmond,* (whilst we had fixtures against *Wasps* and *Rosslyn Park*). Their home ground was in Heston, but the facilities were pretty basic consisting of wooden shacks and no showers. Mike Lakin recalls a match at their airport ground, *'I was in a maul and punches reigned down on me 'from behind' –far from being the enemy it was Harry Masterton-Smith getting a bit over enthusiastic'.* They were also a keen touring club, travelling to the West Country and the Channel Islands. They also took part in the ASCA tournament where they played the likes of Air Lingus, KLM and Air France. During the late 1970's and early 1980's they were at their strongest, regularly fielding up to five teams. Today they play in RFU Herts/Middx. league 3.

Southern Railway RFC
Played 17: Won 7, Lost 7, Cancelled/unrecorded 3
Cook's historical link with Southern Railways is a strong one. The company had become part of the Wagon-Lits Group, whose assets had been frozen when war was declared. The business then became under the management of Southern Railways in 1940. Their rugby club had been established in the 1920's, and their ground in South West London at Raynes Park. They were one of our earlier fixtures from the first 1953/4 season, (and first win 16-3) in which Roy Bannister recalls a convivial after match singing and drinking session in the *Raynes Park Tavern,* an old Victorian pub on the corner opposite the station –a short walk from their ground. At one point in the evening a Salvation Army collector came into the pub seeking funds for their good cause and initially she was largely ignored by the carousing players. Then two strapping forwards came towards her and placing themselves alongside lifted her effortlessly to a nearby table. Then taking her collection tin, proceeded to

collect funds from all present, -everyone contributed. The tin now full they lifted her down and she went on her way. The scene left a vivid impression, who says all forwards are 'hard'. When I joined Cook's in 1959 this was my first fixture in 'club' rugby (we lost 6-19). Cook's also invited the club to play our Dutch visitors RC Hilversum during their Easter tour in 1959. We continued with fixtures until 1962/3, with scores about even. They too found player recruitment an issue and in 1972 merged with *Raynes Park Old Boys* forming the new club *Raynes Park RFC*. They continue to play at their ground in Taunton Avenue, and play in RFU Surrey league 2.

Standard Bank of South Africa RFC
Played 1: Won 1, Cancelled 1

The Standard Bank, who had an established rugger club in Elmers End Road, Beckenham since the 1920's, was founded in South Africa, Cape Province in 1862. It was prominent in financing the development of the diamond fields of Kimberley, and later extended its network further north to the new town of Johannesburg when gold was discovered there. In our only fixture in 1960 we won 5-0 at home. We also played in the Eastern Bank Sevens tournament held at their ground. In 1965 they merged with the *Bank of West Africa*, (our two fixtures against this bank were cancelled) expanding its operations into Cameroon, Gambia, Ghana, Nigeria and Sierra Leone. These banks traditionally encouraged sports, and built some handsome clubhouses and ground facilities. The story goes that when an overseas bank was recruiting new staff, a typical telex request to London would be something along the lines of *'send a left-arm spin bowler and a scrum half'* – it was taken for granted that all other business skills would be in place. The bank merged with Chartered Bank in 1969 forming the Standard Chartered Group.

Sun Alliance RFC
Played 6: Won 1, Lost 4, Cancelled 1
Both the First and 'A' teams had matches against this club between 1959 and 1964, losing most of them. One of the country's oldest assurance companies, Sun was established in 1710, and merged with Alliance in 1959. The *Sun Alliance* ground playing field was at Raynes Park, in south London. Eventually the ground was sold for development to Barratt's Homes. They moved to Horsham in Sussex in 1970, where the new *Sun Alliance Sports & Social Club* was located, and the club became Sunallon RFC. In 1996 following a merger with the Liverpool based Royal Insurance it became *Royal & Sun Alliance RFC.* The company changed to RSA in 2008. After their move to Sussex, the club was eventually to loose its company funding, so became the independent *Holbrook RFC* in 2004. Today they play in RFU Sussex league 1.

Whatever became of...
...a summary of other clubs and their fate

Cook's XV's like many others were playing in a changing world. It was becoming increasingly difficult to recruit new players. Many of our opponents were in the same position. Established clubs with house, college or school affiliations traditionally had 'closed' membership to their own associates. This was making recruitment difficult and through force of necessity many became 'open clubs' – that is open to all comers. This change of policy was designed to attract new players, and most of the clubs we played had, by the early 1970's become open clubs. This helped some of them prosper and survive but others like ourselves ceased playing or merged with other clubs.

Bank of England RFC is thriving. One of our earliest fixtures in 1953, founded in 1886 as a nomadic side, but managed to secure a ground in 1908. One of London's oldest clubs, today they have a *'first-class'* 42 acre prestigious ground and clubhouse in Roehampton (the envy of less fortunate clubs playing in *'economy'*). They play in RFU London 3 N.W. league.

Decca, was a 'house' club we played eight times, winning only twice, and had their home ground in Tolworth Surrey. **Old Masonians,** we played only once, winning 38-3 at Ravensbourne. Their home ground was Home Park, Surrey. In 1966 they merged with Decca to form a new club *Antlers RFC*. Then in 1981 the club became *Antlers-Teddington RFC*, finally changing to just *Teddington RFC* in 1998. Today, they play in RFU London 3 SW league.

Ealing RFC, *(est.1871)* we only managed one game in November 1955 (drawing 6-6 at Ravensbourne against their 'C' XV). A few years earlier this team included the journalist and author Michael Green, who later went on to write about his experiences in *'The Art of Coarse Rugby'*. They are now known as *Ealing Trailfinders RFC*, sponsored by Mike Gooley the ex SAS officer's travel company. Ironically, he only started his successful (and now iconic) business in 1970 after a travel enquiry to Thomas Cook about an overland journey to Katmandu –only to be told *'they didn't do that sort of thing'*. (Surely some mistake?) Today the club is thriving, including women's and mini sections. They play in RFU National league 2 South.

Hermits RFC, we managed two games against them (won and lost). They were formed in 1957 by a group of old boys of St Joseph's Academy, Blackheath. As they were unable to secure agreement from the school Headmaster, they formed a team independent from the Old Boys Association naming it *Hermits RFC*, (after the Hermit crab, which spends most of its life using other creature's shells as its home). They were 'wanderers' until they eventually found a home at Hall Place Playing fields, Bexley. (The rent was a staggering £14 for the season, which had to be borrowed from a player's uncle). When Bexley became a Greater London Borough it was decided to re-name the Club *'Bexley Rugby Football Club'*. The (Hermit) crab was not forgotten and the second team, are still known as the 'Hermits'. They now play in RFU Kent 2 league.

Old Cestrians, we played three away games, winning the first and the 'A' team loosing the others. The club was established in 1952 by the old boys from Cheshunt Grammar school. In 1966 they became *Cheshunt RFC*, and today, they play in RFU London league 3 NW.

Old Isleworthians, only the first XV played them and lost both games during the 1960/61 season. They had been formed in 1957 by a Maths teacher from Isleworth Grammar school, who dreamed up the idea whilst staying at a hotel in Obwalden on a school summer trip to Switzerland. They play in the RFU Herts. & Middx. league 2.

P.L.A, the Port of London Authority, another 'house' club –we played just two fixtures (won and lost). Originally they were known as the Ravens, and established in 1875. They changed their name when to the PLA when it was established in 1909. However, when their Ilford ground was sold for redevelopment in 1991, they reverted to the *Ravens RFC* name, playing at the Ford's Sports ground, in RFU Essex Merit Tables.

Sudbury Court merged with *London Springboks* in 2001, forming *Sudbury & London Springboks* playing in RFU Herts & Middx league 4. In 2010 they plan a merger with *Hayes RFC*.

Finally, **CAV** closed 1988. **Firestone** ceased playing when their plant in Brentford closed in 1980. **Juno** closed in 1969. **Meadhurst** -British Petroleum closed in 1991 (it's now just a fitness/lifestyle club), and **RAMS** closed in 1989.

Seven a side competitions

Cook's regularly took part in seven-a-side competitions during the late 1950's and early 1960's –although no records survive. The following are some photos of an inter-department competition in April 1958.

(Photos Hugh Dalzell)
Winners: (8-6) HTD -Holiday Tour Dept, Berkeley Street,
standing *left to right*: Derek Bascombe, John Usher, Graham Block,
Geoff Wilson, Brian Wright,
sitting: Brian Davies, Bill Trenfield, Hugh Dalzell

Runners up: London Offices,
standing *left to Right* : Pete Dawson, Mike Lidbetter,
Roy Bannister, (☺?), sitting: Malcolm McCalla, (☺?), John Carter,

7. Hilversum Easter Tours

'Do you like action and can you take a beating? Then with rugby you have a lot of fun. Rugby is a fantastic sport where you definitely do not have to be macho'. 'Everybody is most welcome to join the Rugby Club Hilversum, a club with a big number of Nationalities.'
R C Hilversum Website

The Dutch have been playing rugby since the early 1930's, and in 1932 some six months after their national team had played their first match against Belgium, the Dutch Rugby Union was founded. The Rugby Club in Hilversum was established in the 1950's with players like Frits Frankfort, Cor de Rie and Karel van Spengen, at much the same time as the resurrected Thos Cook RFC. It was amongst a dozen or so clubs in Holland that established the basis of Dutch rugby after the war.

Rowley Hope was an enigmatic Cook's player, (Roy Bannister remembers *'he just used to appear on Saturdays and then just as soon disappear again'*) through his contacts arranged for the club's first overseas tour to Hilversum, Holland, in 1958. This was something innovative at the time as most clubs would usually select a domestic tour to the West Country for example. The side was captained by Don Keston and included such stalwart names as, Hugh Dalzell, Roy Bannister, Pete Shaw, Romeo Bazzali with Derek Bascombe doing some refereeing; the tour was a great success. These exchange visits became a regular fixture after the first tour match and continued for about seven seasons. The same year one of our early English fixture opponents, *Great Western Railways XV* was also making their first tour to Holland, playing against *AAC-Amsterdam* as well as *RC Hilversum*.

The first tour in 1958

The first overseas tour to Holland at Easter 1958 was also accompanied by the Cook's Sports Club Honorary

General Secretary A.J. (Andy) Anderson as a spectator. He wrote an article of his experiences for the May/June issue of the Staff Magazine, under the title *'Dank U, Bosbokken'*. This is an extract. The touring party, (department/office in brackets) originally 30, now reduced to 29 as one member Rowley Hope was mysteriously AWOL (missing).

Derek Bascombe (Post Order Dept.)

John Usher (Holiday Tours)

Dennis Beal (Post Order Dept.)

Vic Bulmer-Jones (Passports)

Don Keston (Post Order Dept.) (Captain)

John Carter (Leadenhall Street)

Fred Petts (Post Order Dept.)

Peter Davies (Coding)

Derek Sells (Post Order Dept.)

Tony Golds (I.I.T)
+ girl friend Rosemary ?

Romeo Bazzali (Forwarding House)

Fred Jenkins (Uniformed Staff) + wife Maureen

Ron Barrowman (Foreign Exchange)

Ivor Jenkins (Fred's brother) + wife 'Pinky'

Bob Maidment (Foreign Exchange)

Mike Lidbetter (Kensington)

Keith McCarthy (Foreign Exchange)

Peter Shaw (Rates)

Roy Bannister (Harrods)

Willie Trenfield (Winter Sports)

John Boden (Publicity) + wife Carol

Andy Anderson (Hon. Gen. Sec. Sports Club)

Brian Davies (Holiday Tours)

Rosemary Chown & Rosemary Newton (girl-friends)

Hugh Dalzell (Holiday Tours)

Thursday 3rd April

The appointed assembly point was Platform 9 Liverpool Street Station on for the start of the club's first tour to Holland. Derek Bascombe had made all the arrangements and much to the surprise of the Holiday Tours contingent (Andy's in-house joke) the compartments on the 7.30pm train were actually reserved as stated. The train journey (during which they enjoyed many aperitifs –Andy said 'a couple') was to connect with the overnight sailing by (a new ship) the *SS Amsterdam* on the Harwich to Hook crossing, arriving in Holland early morning the next day. The train journey from Hook to Hilversum via Utrecht was remarkable efficient with spotless compartments (the cleanliness was remarked on frequently) but the compartments very hot –it seems the Dutch like to keep themselves warm, and likewise in their homes, with huge coal-burning stoves. The group arrived in Hilversum early morning and were met by the welcoming committee of *RC Hilversum* at the station an taken to a local restaurant for coffee where the Cook players were given a copy of their club magazine *'Die Bosbock'* which thoughtfully had been written in English giving the day-by-day itinerary and events. The group moved on to the Hilversum Clubhouse *'De Jonge Graaf van Burren'* a splendid 16th century building with a magnificent interior with dark wooden panel walls, white ceiling with black beams and a large brick fireplace with the inevitable stove. The highly polished floor shone like glass and all around there were displays of old historical weapons, drums, muskets, cutlasses, pewter pots and old china delft-ware which coupled with the subdued lighting created a cosy atmosphere and social effect, all the more pleasurable as it was completely unexpected.

Friday 4th April

After lunch the Cook's group travelled to Amsterdam for a little sightseeing as the Dutch hosts were working in their day-jobs – Good Friday is not regarded as a general holiday in Holland. Most of the party were accommodated in player's homes but a few with wives and girl friends stayed in the *Hotel Hiench*. The evening was spent enjoying a drink or two with their new hosts.

Saturday 5th April

This was a match day in the afternoon, so the morning was spent exploring the town of Hilversum. The impression that everyone agreed on, was that it was a very attractive place and again, spotlessly clean. The modern shops with attractive and helpful assistants selling perfumes, electrical razors, cigarette lighters and cigars were found to be so much cheaper than England. The afternoon match was at 3pm against a *Hilversum 'A' XV* played on a soccer pitch with rugby posts attached to the goal frame, as soccer is much more popular in Holland than rugby.

RC Hilversum (Holland) v Thos. Cook & Son's RFC
Saturday 5th April 1958
Line up: Hilversum 'A' (left) Capt. 'Frits' Frankfort, Referee, Thos. Cook (right) *Left to right*: Don Keston, Romeo Bazzali, Pete Shaw, Roy Bannister, (☺?)

The opponents were a lively team but lacked the strength and experience of *Cook's XV* and we won against them with the final score 33-0. Derek Bascombe refereed.

The scorers were as follows:
Mike Lidbetter -3 tries (9)
Peter Shaw – 1 try (3) and 1 conversion (2) (5)
Don Keston – 2 conversions (4)
Hugh Dalzell – 1 drop goal (3)
Keith McCarthy -1 try (3)
John Carter – 1 try (3)
Ivor Jenkins – 1 try (3)
(Points add up to 30 – so a discrepancy somewhere?)

The game was greatly enjoyed by both teams and our opponents deserve every praise for taking their defeat (or thrashing as it would be known in England) in such a sporting manner. The evening was spent at the Hilversum clubhouse celebrating the win and joining in with the Dutch sing song. During the evening the hosts showed a short cine-film of a very novel tug-of-war they had had introduced the year before. The rope stretched across the Hilversum canal, which is about forty to fifty yards wide, and two teams tug against each other from opposite banks. *Hilversum* was successful against three local teams and spectators enjoyed the wetting which the losing teams received.

Sunday 6th April
This was *Der Tag* as the day became known, playing against their senior team. The afternoon match was to be played at *Agovv Football Club* at Apeldoorn. The team left in the morning by coach travelling via Amersfoort to see the Royal Palace, and stopping for some coffee and sandwiches. The nerves of some of the Cook players had been rather shattered when they were informed that the game was to be televised. Outside the ground there were posters advertising an International match between *Bosbokken (Hilversum)* and *Cooksons (London)*. This was all new, and the team learnt that the film would be shown in local cinemas

and on TV the following week! (Hugh Dalzell recalls the team's nerves and Ivor Jenkins calming everyone down). Inside the ground there were about 2,500 spectators present when both teams lined up for the National Anthems. We soon realised we were up against very stiff opposition. Although they lacked some the finer arts of Scrumaging, they were very fast, superbly fit and excellent in the tackle. It was a close match with the opening score by *Hilversum* scoring a try which their hooker failed to convert. Half time still 0-3. The second half opened with a penalty to *Hilversum* which they failed to convert, and we then failed with two penalty attempts at long distance. With about fifteen minutes to go we were again awarded a penalty. Don Keston 'teed up' and kicked hard and true, this time the ball just scraping over the bar, it was 3-3 draw! Both sides went at it 'hammer and tongs' but at the final whistle the score remained at a draw. It was a good result to a really excellent and hard fought game. On the way back to Hilversum we stopped at the *Prinses Juliana Toren* a large wayside

Cook's XV Sunday 6th April 1958   (Photo Wim Van Spengen)
Standing L/R: Derek Bascombe, John Usher, Tony Gold, Jock Barrowman, Mike Lidbetter, Don Keston, Fred Jenkins, Ivor Jenkins, Pete Shaw, Vic Bulmer-Jones, Kneeling L/R: (☺?), Bob Maidment, Bill Trenfield, Hugh Dalzell, John Carter, Romeo Bazzali

Bosbokken (Hilversum) and Cooksons (London) *(sic)*
Sunday 6th April 1958 (at Apeldoorn) pre-match line up: RC
Hilversum (right –extreme right 'Frits' Frankfort) Thos. Cook (left)
Right to left: Derek Bascombe (referee-white shorts), Hugh Dalzell,
Pete Shaw, Mike Lidbetter, and rest of team

restaurant for a good hot meal, afterwards enjoying the
attached fun-fair rides for an hour or so. Back in
Hilversum, the tired but nevertheless jubilant party
celebrated in style at the club house.

Easter **Monday** 7th April
In the morning the group left by coach for Amsterdam
for a privately chartered launch to tour the canals and
waterways,

(Photos Hugh Dalzell)
Cook's (left) enjoying the sights and Hilversum (right) the beer!

returning to Hilversum and the *De Jonge Graaf van Burren* for the last time and for lunch. Almost before we knew where we were – and many players didn't –we were on our way to the station, with a mighty crowd of players, spectators and friends. On the platform singing *'Auld Lang Syne'* with final farewells, until our new-made friends became a blur in the distance.

Andy Anderson concluded: *'This was the first tour for the (rugby) section and I speak for all members when I say there will never be a happier one. It is difficult to find words adequate to express our thanks for the hospitality and friendship which were bestowed on us. We hope that they will be coming to England so that we may have* the *opportunity to repay the many kindnesses shown us'* -and they did. The pattern was now set for the following years. Each club took it in turns to act as host venue.

RC Hilversum first visit to Ravensbourne in 1959

The following year the Hilversum teams were guest visitors to Ravensbourne during the Easter week-end in 1959. The programme was prepared and printed, for the match on Sunday 29th March 1959. It explained: *'Today we have great pleasure in entertaining the Hilversum RFC who are the reigning Dutch champions. Rugby Football is still almost unknown in Holland but there are about 12 pioneer clubs who play each other frequently, and as often as possible most teams from the British Forces in Holland, Belgium and Germany. Hilversum is captained by Feike (Frits) Frankfort, a lively little scrum-half with a good knowledge of the game. Frankfort, like several of the side, has been capped for Holland in Internationals against Belgium and Germany. The Dutchmen play a fast open game of Rugby; therefore we hope that everyone will see an enjoyable game this afternoon.'*

The game was set for kick-off at 3.15 pm and the teams selected as follows:

Thos Cook's XV			FC Hilversum XV
Blue, Gold & Chocolate		- Colours -	Blue & White Hoops
1	R. Bazzali	Full Back	Gert van Reenen
2	R. Gillies	Wing Threequarter	H. Giel
3	M. Lidbetter	Centre Threequarter	C. van Essen
4	P. Shaw	Centre Threequarter	Aart Baartwijk
5	B. Davies	Wing Threequarter	Wessel Tabak
6	H. Dalzell (Capt)	Fly Half	Cor de Rie
7	J. Carter	Scrum Half	Feike Frankfort (Capt)
8	G. Mos	Prop Forward	J. de Loos
9	B. Martin	Hooker	J. Kaljee
10	R. Bannister	Prop Forward	G. Lam
11	P. Simmonds	Second Row	P. Waiboer
12	D. Keston	Second Row	L. Vonno
13	D. Isaac	Wing Forward	Henk van Willigenburg
14	W. Ashby	Lock Forward	J. Koppel
15	J. Usher	Wing Forward	Jan van Altenna

The officials were: Referee: Mr. G.A. Lamidey (Kent Society), Touch Judges: Mr. D. Bascombe (Thos. Cook & Son) and Mr. G. Van Zal (Hilversum). Cook's winning 6-3.

Easter 1959 Ravensbourne, Left: **RC Hilversum (visitors)**
Right: **Thos Cook & Son RFC XV** *Cook players: Rear left to right*: Pete Shaw, Pete Simmonds, John Usher, Dave Isaac, Don Keston, Mike Lidbetter, 'Pincher' Martin *Front left to right:* Hugh Dalzell, John Carter, Romeo Bazzali, P.Gillies, W.Ashby, Brian Davies, Roy Bannister, Gary Mos

Hugh Dalzell presenting trophy to Hilversum Captain Frits Frankfort, Gert van Reenen -extreme right   (Photo Hugh Dalzell)

Ravensbourne clubhouse 1959: ('house' band far left), Dutch visitors, (all wearing ties, blazers and badges), Aart Baatwijk being 'affectionate', to Derek Bascombe –only because he had the beer jug!

Ravensbourne clubhouse 1959: some members of RC Hilversum in the bar. Everybody wore ties and blazers then. The reason they looked so glum – they were drinking out of HALF PINTS mugs! Although Karel van Spengen (extreme left) is beginning to see the 'joke'.

Earlier the same weekend on the 27th April Hilversum also played against one of our regular fixture opponents at home –a Southern Railways XV played at Ravensbourne, no record of the score survived, except the following photos.

Hilversum with opponents Southern Railway XV (Photo Hugh Dalzell)
Ravensbourne April 1959

Roy Bannister recalls one Dutch player the diminutive 'Frits' Frankfort as being one of the touring party comedians. On one occasion after arriving at the Horse Guards in Whitehall during the sightseeing tour of London the little 'Frits' leapt into the guard box and stood to attention just after one of the guards had started his march, creating a photo opportunity as a 'souvenir'.

RC Hilversum sightseeing in London 1959: (Photo Wim Van Spengen) Left to Right: Karel Van Spengen, Aart Baartwijk, Frits Frankfort (with Cook's Bear), Gert van Reenen, ☺?

The second tour to Hilversum in April 1960

I was lucky enough to be selected for the tour in 1960, and was the culmination of my first playing season with the club. I no doubt had impressed the selection team, as I had already played a few matches for the first team, scoring a few tries during the season. It was also to be my first flight. The club had chartered an Eagle Airways 'Vickers Viking' aircraft -this was a 24-seater aircraft, derived from the war-time Wellington bomber. British Eagle International (as it became later) had been formed earlier in 1948 by Harold Bamberg, a former wartime pilot. The airline expanded from charter work into scheduled services operating internal UK flights and into Western Europe, but went into

(images courtesy of Britisheagle.net)

liquidation in 1968. The glut of aircraft in the market in during the 1950's meant that charters could be had for something like half a crown a mile (25p in new money). This type of aircraft had done sterling work during the post war Berlin Airlift. (Where another wartime pilot Freddie Laker, who became an aviation entrepreneur founding his low cost 'Skytrain' service to the USA in the 1970's).

Friday 15th April
We checked in at London Heathrow in the evening and were bussed out to the aircraft on the rain-soaked tarmac. As we walked towards it, because of its small tail wheel, the aircraft slopped towards the rear, a typical military plane –which it had been originally. On entering we shuffled in file upward along the narrow centre aisle and had to literally step over the wing span mountings that came through the cabin fuselage. We flew to Amsterdam Schipol airport after a noisy and bumpy flight with occasional disconcerting flashes of flames from the engines, during which I had recourse to the ubiquitous brown paper bag. Amongst the touring side were a number of non playing supporters including Dennis Beal who'd been on the earlier tour, and Jill, Dave Isaac's blond haired wife. Dave and Jill were inseparable, who were both friendly and showed me a lot of kindness. It came as a considerable shock some years later to learn that Dave who had by then

left the company, and working for Wakefield Fortune in London still a young man, had suddenly died.

On arrival in Holland after custom formalities, a coach transferred us to Hilversum where we were to meet the officials and opposition players in their clubhouse. To keep expenses down (as in the first tour) many of the Hilversum club members arranged to accommodate individual players of our team for the duration of the tour. I was to stay with Jan Rosman, who was much the same age but had limited, English (and I of course spoke no Dutch). His mother made me very welcome. She too spoke little English, but during my stay would always tune in the BBC news on the radio each morning at breakfast. I learnt later from Jan's older brother that during World War Two she had hid escaping allied airmen from the Germans, and used to do the same for them on a secret radio. Unfortunately Jan was not selected for the Hilversum team so I didn't get an opportunity to play against him. *RC Hilversum* takes its name from the same town which is about 30km south-east of Amsterdam, surrounded by heathland, woods, meadows, lakes, and smaller villages. More interestingly perhaps to British people is its radio station. The Dutch often call it *'media city'* as it is the principal centre for radio and television broadcasting in the Netherlands. Radio Netherlands, heard worldwide via shortwave radio since the 1920s, is based here. As a result many old radio sets in Britain had a *'Hilversum'* dial position marked on their tuning scales (along with other exotic locations like *'Athlone'* *'Luxembourg'* and *'Belgrade'* –which some older readers might remember from growing up in the '40's and '50's).

Saturday 16th April

In the morning we were taken on a tour of the Heineken Brewery. The old building, built on a site that had brewed beer since the 16th century, was located in Stadhouderskade, in the heart of Amsterdam, just east of the famous Rijksmuseum. It had been bought by a member of the Heineken family in 1867, the beer that still bears his name. We enjoyed the tour experiencing the sights and smells of the beer's ingredients and processes, in anticipation of a glass of the freshly-poured pilsner in the tasting room. As a number of us were not picked for the afternoon's match we could enjoy the Dutch hospitality all the more, which of course we did. This old brewery ceased production in 1988, and the building was converted into what tourist visitors know as the *'Heineken Experience,'* where you can learn about the history of one of the world's most recognizable beer brands and of course taste the famous Dutch pilsner, during an inter-active ninety minute tour. Today, it is sponsor of the Heineken Cup, professional rugby's successful European knock out competition. Another popular Amsterdam brewed beer at the time was Amstel, the brewery founded in the 19th century, but was eventually taken over by Heineken in 1968.

Easter Tour Hilversum (Holland) April 1960,
Some of the team and supporters relaxing in Amsterdam, outside Royal Palace, *Standing left to right*: Dutch(☺?), English supporter (☺?), George Davies, Dutch(☺?), *Kneeling left to right*: Romeo Bazzali, Jan Rosman (Dutch), Dennis Beal (supporter), Marcus Wade, Dutch(☺?)

A match had been arranged against *Rugby Club 't Gooi,* in Naarden, a provincial town in the North of Holland. It was once the old 14th century capital of Holland, part of the Spanish Netherlands, with a good example of a Spanish star fort, complete with fortified walls and a moat, some 26 km from Amsterdam's Schipol airport. This is  one of the oldest established clubs, founded in 1933 by some enthusiastic Delft students, and has been in the forefront of Dutch rugby ever since. (Photo of Hugh Dalzell, Cook's Captain exchanging the traditional club flag and receiving an enamel jug –inscribed *'bier is best'* –see photo). Today, the club is still thriving and has over 200 members. The match was eventually won 14 – 6. Like most after-match get together they often pass as a blur - well they certainly do forty years later, and this was no exception.

Sunday 17th April

This was the day for the main match, and I was selected to play open side wing forward. Below is a copy of the original playing list which our hosts had typed out. The match against RC Hilversum was set for the afternoon. It was made into an occasion with a local band and something like a 1000 spectators in the stand and lining the touch line. This was very nerve racking as the most I had played in front of was a just few of the team's girl friends loyally stamping their feet against the cold for the odd match. We lined up (something we never did in club games) for the country anthems. I experienced the 'butterflies' of anticipation before kick-off, which disappear immediately the game starts.

Rugby Club Hilversum Opstellingen R.C. Thos Cook

Achterspeler: *Gerard Zomer,*
Driekwarten: *Aart Baartwijk, Gert van Rhenen,*
John Broekhuis, Ad Hazelaar,
Halven: *Pim Ooms, 'Frits' Frankfort,*
Voorwaartsen: (Back Row) *Wessel Tabak, Jan Kaljee,*
Jaap Smallenburg,
(Second row) *Henk van Willigenburg, Jan van Altenna,*
(Front row) *Piet Waiboer, Cor de Rie, Jan de Loos*

Full back: *Romeo Bazzali*
Threequarters: *Brian Davies, Peter Shaw, Mike Lidbetter,*
Brian Wright,
Halves: *Hugh Dalzell, Bob Maidment*
Forwards: (Back row) *John Dann, Dave Isaac, Keith McCarthy*
(Second row) *Bill Briddock, Brian Smith,*
(Front row) *Jack New, Mark Wade, Brian Dewdney*

Thos. Cook & Son's RFC XV after winning (13-9) at Hilversum
Standing left to right: Brian Davies, Brian Dewy, Dave Isaac, Bill
Briddock, Brian Wright, Mike Lidbetter, Pete Shaw, Brian Smith,
Jack New, *Kneeling: left to right*: Marcus Wade, John Dann, Keith
McCarthy, Hugh Dalzell, Bob Maidment, Romeo Bazzali

Author, as wing forward, (age 16¾)   The Hilversum band
clutching 'après match' beer

This day I realised the match would be taken very seriously –after all we were representing the company abroad! I remember little of the actual game but I do remember having never tackled harder or continued at such pace in my whole playing career. My opposite number in the Dutch scrum was *Wessel Tabak,* who had the habit of holding on to my shirt (illegally) after I broke from the scrum, as my target was *Pim Ooms* the Hilversum fly half. In the end it took the odd quiet thump on his arm to break his habit. (Unfortunately this was seen by the referee, Derek Bascombe, who had a quiet word in my ear for that un-sporting gesture on tour). Mike Lidbetter remembers instead of oranges or lemons –Hilversum provided half-time bread rolls with cheese or ham! However, despite this 'added weight' the result was a victory to Cook's 13 – 9. The evening passed in a blur, again, thanks to Dutch hospitality. Although I can dimly recall the Dutch singing incomprehensible songs, except for the odd words we could recognise like 'Heineken beer', repeating this easily in unison. Later that evening, I also have a vague recollection of hearing that someone had ridden a bicycle into the Hilversum canal.

Monday 18th April

Today, the end of the tour, we are scheduled to fly home from Schipol. To help sooth our hangovers enroute to the airport the coach took us to visit the Keukenhof flower garden, near the town of Lisse, some 15 miles south of Amsterdam. The Dutch are proud of this park as it had been created just ten years previously. We were told it was originally part of the estate of Jacoba van Beieren Keukenhof. It had subsequently passed to a rich merchant family, who commissioned landscape architects, (they had also designed the Vondelpark in Amsterdam), to create an English landscape garden around their house. The idea of the flower gardens came from the local mayor together with a number of leading bulb growers and exporters in 1949, who wanted to create an open air flower exhibition for their products. The garden is only open for a short period in the spring of each year, so it coincided with our April tour. Millions of hand-planted bulbs are scattered throughout the estate to create the world's largest flower garden. We probably didn't do it justice or quite appreciate the experience then, although I do remember the beautiful flowers. Today its reputation amongst gardeners has grown (no pun intended) and now draws great numbers of visitors from all over the world.

The following seasons 1961 - 1964

In April 1961 Hilversum returned to play us at Ravensbourne. It was my turn to offer hospitality and Jan stayed with my family in Kingsbury North London. We would travel by tube and rail to Ravensbourne for the matches of which there seem to be no result records although the following photos survive. At the end of Jan's stay, as we were leaving the house he turned and spoke to my mother in faltering English saying *'Dank U for the eats and sleeps'* much to her amusement. She remembered his politeness for many years.

Playing Hilversum created many friendships, I sadly lost touch with Jan Rosman, but Mike Lidbetter recalls later, spending several holidays with Gert van Reenen their full back when he ran a pub in Amersfoort. Karel van Spengen's son Wim as an excited ten year old remembers his father returning from the 1964 tour with pictures of the Beatles –unobtainable in Holland at the time. Late that year, he and his family returned enjoying a Christmas visit to Bob Maidment and family in London.

Easter 1961 Ravensbourne,
RC Hilversum (their Line Out) against Cook's First XV *TC players left to right:* extreme left- Bob Maidment, *(scrum half)*, (☺?), (☺?), (☺?), Derek Bascombe *(referee-white shorts)*, *(Forwards)*, Gary Mos, Dave Isaac, Harry Masterton-Smith, (☺?), (☺?)

Harry Masterton-Smith recalls the RC Hilversum visit, *'two images stand out from the Hilversum visit in '61. One was of the wives and girl friends in the bar, where they all sang heartily in Dutch or English, except that the Dutch girls blushed furiously when we sang in Dutch, and the English girls likewise when we sang in English. The other was of the farewell at Liverpool Street Station. We were all allowed onto the departure platform and proceeded to perform a range of songs (mostly in Dutch) – 'a cappella' (unaccompanied) and with full harmonies. We finished with a rendition of "Ik bin der*

Musikmeister" which brought an enthusiastic round of applause from the whole station'.

Easter 1961 Ravensbourne RC Hilversum visitors
(their line out - our scrum) against Cook's 'A' XV
(Sequence of photo's taken by girlfriend supporters)

Left to right: 1ˢᵗ photo: (Forwards) Dave Keeling (*Hooker*), Dave Isaac, Geoff Brooks, Vic Bulmer-Jones, (ref: white shorts), (Wing☺?), John Dann (scrum half), *2ⁿᵈ photo:* jumping: Derek Sells (*Capt*), Pete Davies, (Wing☺?), John Dann, (Scrum half),

-another 'tactical' put-in to give Dave Keeling a 'competitive'
advantage!

1963

For some reason no fixture had been arranged for Easter 1962. The following year Robin Garrett remembers travelling with the Cook's touring team playing a game against some other Dutch sides (names lost in memory, although it might have been Delft or Leiden universities) as well as the established

Hilversum fixture. He too recalls the Dutch hospitality, and on the homeward journey the overnight ferry sailing from Hook van Holland to Harwich was delayed whilst our Dutch hosts were encoring their many goodbyes onboard. Sadly no records or photos survive.

1964

By 1964 it was our turn to host Hilversum again at Ravensbourne. I had agreed to accommodate a player but this time my original Dutch host Jan Rosman had disappeared from the visitors touring party, so I was allocated another Dutch player whose name escapes me, but my wife thinks it might have been Ben. By this time the sixties were well and truly swinging and I had acquired a tiny flat in Pimlico (in a house that was once the home of the inventor of Lawn Tennis, Major Walter Wingfield) which I shared with another Cook's employee, Mike Edmunds. We'd met on a 'Bob' Shilling travel training course in Berkeley Street, and he was based at the Cook's office, near the Strand Palace Hotel. He was not a rugby man –but he graciously arranged to stay with his parents in Haslemere over Easter whilst I entertained our Dutch guest (we only had two beds). The 1963-64 records show that on 28th March the first XV drew 0-0 with Hilversum and the 'A' XV lost to their 'A' side 0-3 at Ravensbourne, unfortunately, the after match activities of this tour are another forty-years-on memory blur.

1965

There was one last tour to Holland before the club closed the following year – but sadly no records survive. Except that is, some photos kindly supplied by Wim, the son of Karel van Spangen one of the founder members of Hilversum rugby club.

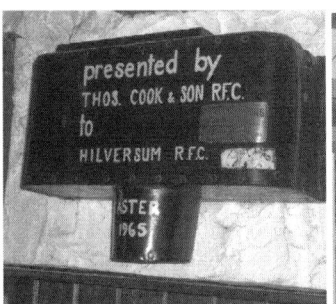

Toilet cistern presented to
Hilversum Easter 1965

The bar at Hilversum
clubhouse c.1960's

Ravensbourne toilet seat taken from Cook's clubhouse
(photos Wim van Spengen)

Giving and taking 'trophies' is very much a rugby tradition. However I learnt the 'liberated' Ravensbourne toilet seat that once graced Hilversum's clubhouse has since been 'repatriated' by a visiting English side – name unknown. Bastards!

RC Hilversum forty years on

Today the club is thriving. It has successfully performed at top level in the Dutch league winning the championship over ten times –and again in 2010. It has grown and now has around 230 members with about 90 youth players together with a complete team of professional coaching staff (how times change). In addition the club has a fully equipped gym and a sauna. There are two playing fields with flood lighting and two bars. The centre of the club is the club-house *De Jonge Graaf van Burren* (no change there then). As the club announces in its website; '*Rugby is still popular in the Netherlands. In England, France, South Africa, and New Zealand Rugby is the favourite sport for years. In their stadiums they have as many supporters as we do for a football match between Ajax and Feyenoord. The first thing an Englishman does with the birth of his son he registers with the local rugby club due to long waiting lists*'. Well a little over the top perhaps, but we can appreciate the sentiment.

When I was eight, I can remember being taken by my uncle to watch the young Cliff Morgan, in his 1951 international debut at fly half at the Arms Park in Cardiff. He went on to be the star of the Lions Tour of South Africa in 1955 becoming a Welsh legend. In May 2009 at the age of 79 years in a rare interview in the Sunday Times, he explained his views on the forthcoming Lions tour to South Africa. Speaking to their rugby correspondent, he said '*...that as well as winning rugby matches, they are (on tour) to share ideas, and the good things in life with their hosts. They will know if they have had a good tour if, at the end of it, they are sad to be leaving*'. This seems to me a good enough expectation for any rugby tour. Those feelings were shared by many who toured with Cook's RFC to Holland, and best summed up by Andy Anderson's original comments of the 1958 tour '*Dank U, Bosbokken*'.

8. Club Social life

'Come, Landlord, fill a flowing bowl, Till' it runn'eth over, For tonight we'll merry, merry, be, For tonight we'll merry, merry, be, Tomorrow we'll be sober!

The original land at Ravensbourne in Kent was acquired in 1903 and by 1904 the ground had been laid, a little sports pavilion built and opened. It provided two football pitches during the winter and four tennis courts, two cricket pitches and a bowling green during the summer. In 1910 the rugby section was formed and a pitch marked out. After the First World War a new and larger pavilion was built in 1922 which was opened by the Club's President, Frank Cook, one of the grandsons' of Thomas. The 1920's were a period of remarkable success with various sections winning many cups and awards. The centre of social activity was the clubhouse, built in a typical (of the time) Edwardian 'Mock-Tudor' style. The ground stretched over several acres alongside the rail line, a short walk from the station down an unmade and unlit road. By rail from central London (Victoria or Charing Cross) the journey takes just 30 minutes. To the rugby XV it was called the 'clubhouse' but to the cricket XI it was the 'pavilion'. During the Second World War the grounds had been requisitioned by the military, and by the fifties it was just coming back into company use. Roy Bannister recalls in the early days of the revived club some nearby company sports ground were occasionally used like *The Times* and *OXO* in Bromley (where in the summer of 1959, a Spitfire with engine failure, put down on their cricket pitch, after a Battle of Britain memorial flight over Whitehall- luckily it was during the tea-interval). By the time of the first RC Hilversum visit the clubhouse was in full swing.

The Ravensbourne Clubhouse (Pavilion)

During the winter season we shared it with other sections –notably association football, and occasional hockey teams. As Harry Masterton-Smith recalls '*Apart from scaring the football teams out of the baths and bar at the clubhouse, the strongest memories are of the post match activities. We had a good singing reputation and a useful darts team, playing for a pint each game. It's amazing how much beer you can get from a kitty when you're winning in the bar'*. The clubhouse had very good facilities (compared with many away venues we played at) which included changing rooms (home and visitors), with wooden bench seats around the walls with hanging pegs for clothes. A full shower system and joy of joys a small deep plunge bath. In the common area was an open plan lounge with the usual dark wood utility tables and chairs, and a red brick fireplace. The curtained windows and half-glass doors opened on to the playing fields, which in summer would have some decorative flower beds edging around the pavilion. Inside a dartboard encased in a mahogany door-frame was located on a wall close to the entrance door.

Ravensbourne Clubhouse 1960/1 season, *Beer and Senior Service cigarettes Left to right*: Derek Sells (*Capt. 'A' XV*), Harry Masterton–Smith, Bobbie Gould, Brian Davies, John Dann, Dave Isaac, back of heads (☺?), Derek Bascombe

On the opposite side a door way led to a small plain rustic bar which had some rugby memorabilia displayed with presentation 'V' shaped flags of overseas clubs we'd played. Marcus Wade who worked for the Irish airline Aer Lingus, used to regale us with stories of the large number of single women flying out to Morocco -looking for love and romance? This was well before the riotous behaviour of Club 18-30 days! (This company is now part of the Thomas Cook Group).

On the inside of the rugby changing room door I recall on one occasion someone (I believe Brian Wright – because he had an eye for a pretty girl) had Sellotaped a 'life-size' magazine photograph of 'Brigitte Bardot' (printed over several pages as a pull-out section). It was a publicity still of her 1962 film, 'A Very Private Affair'. This really did create a life size image (she was only 5' 5") delightfully sexily dressed in a man's shirt. Brigitte would receive appreciative 'pats' by many players as we clattered down the corridor for the field of play. But alas our affair didn't last long.

Ravensbourne Clubhouse Saturday 11th November 1961
Our sartorial statement: '*all wearing ties and occasional cardigans'*.(No 'A' team game that day, the First XV played *Old Isleworthians* losing 0-3) *Standing left to right*: (Roy Bannister, Steve Sutcliffe-Hey, Pete Davies, *Sitting left to right*: Pete Hawkins, John Dann, Derek Sells (*Capt. A XV*), John Lowe, Bobbie Gould, Dave Isaac, & Jill (*wife*), Harry Masterton-Smith, Geoff Brooks

It was taken down between away fixtures by one of the spoil-sport stewards –we suspected Mr Gladdy of *'why was he born so beautiful'* fame.

The Clubhouse was run by a couple, Mr and Mrs Gladdy and occasionally their daughter. Regular club dances were held accompanied by a 'house' band to add to the rhythm of social life. Mrs Gladdy used to provide the food -'dripping on toast' was a favourite as Hugh Dalzell's recalls. There were other stewards and groundsmen as well I believe. Old Mr Gladdy (every adult seems 'old' when you are a teenager), I remember as a slight, rather grumpy and humourless individual. Everything seemed 'filth' to him, from our boots to our songs, typically he would moan *'it's filthy, -all this filth (he meant mud) you bring in on your boots, -and in the (plunge) pool, I've got to clean that lot up, not like the cricket team'*, et cetera. I'm sure Mr Gladdy viewed the rugby section with dread – preferring the 'flannelled fools' who called the clubhouse the Pavilion. However, on the plus side we and our visitors must have kept the Ravensbourne bar profits going. Inevitably at some point he'd receive a playful rendition of *'Why was he born so beautiful, why was he born at all, he's no bloody use to anyone he's no bloody use at all;'* - although, to be fair we would sing this frequently about anyone we considered a 'pain' or who constantly dropped passes- nearly everyone in fact.

Recruitment and Training

Each season in September there would be a series of trial games so the club captains could assess the playing strengths and abilities of existing as well as new players. Some new players were not that committed and often as the season drew on would make excuses for not being able to play. One excuse which stands out in memory for its sheer absurdity was given as follows: *'...it had been raining and I was standing under a shop blind, when all of a suddenly it gave way, and the collected rainwater drenched me, I had to go home'*. I recall Derek Sells saying on several occasions, the only excuse for not being available to play *'was death'*. Michael Green, a humorist, wrote *'The Art of Coarse Rugby'* in 1960 which immediately struck a cord with those that read it. (I was given a copy as a Christmas present). One of his descriptions of the game stated *'A game played by fewer than fifteen a side, at least half of whom should be totally unfit'*. In fact there were some new players in the 'A' team that didn't actually know there were fifteen in a full team. On one rare occasion watching the ball pass successfully man to man along our attacking three-quarter line, only to see the winger pass it perfectly (and unaccountably), into touch! Without realising it then, the 'writing was on the wall' for the club.

RUGBY AGAIN SOON

ONCE again the strident cries of the all valiant forwards and flying feet of the threes will disturb the gentle calm of Ravensbourne when the rugby section take up their training sessions on Tuesday evenings.

As we shall be fielding two XV's next season on all possible occasions, may we make a special request to rugby enthusiasts to " come and join us ? " Gentlemen wishing to take up the sport will be extended a warm welcome and every encouragement.

Training will kick-off on Tuesday, July 31st and continue until our first match on September 22nd versus the Bank of London and South America at Ravensbourne.

D. BASCOMBE

P.O.D.

There was very little actual training outside the game itself particularly in the 'A' team. Usually in July/August issue of the staff magazine there would be a reminder about rugby training at Ravensbourne. From time to time there were various demands and exhortations for London based members to attend the Tuesday evening sessions at the Lucas Tooth Gym in Tooley Street for circuit training. Hugh recalls it was led by an ex Royal Navy PT instructor, and found the training completely knackering! Mike Lidbetter remembers him as a slightly mad Irishman. Roy Bannister also attended, but then he was a First XV stalwart, however I must admit only attending once. Tooley Street is located in Bermondsey between London and Tower Bridges. That part of the south bank in the 1950's and 1960's was full of old dark narrow cobbled streets, warehouses and wharfs (hardly changed from Dickens's time) and not the 'gentrified' area it is today. It was popular with boxers, their corner-men and hangers on and quite frankly it was spooky –this was still the London of the Richardson and Kray underworld gangs. The nearest I managed to this regular exercise stopped short at the *George* in Borough High Street, with its simple ground floor rooms and bars, (the latticed windows, black-beams, bare floorboards,-spooky enough for me) to enjoy an after-office pint of Fullers London Pride with Bobby Gould. However using the gym had other benefits, our match secretary Hugh Dalzell was able to secure a new fixture with *Old Olavians,* a club who were formed in the 1950's as old boys of St Olaves School which was also based in Tooley Street. At that time they were 'wanderers' and the first team played them in the autumn of 1959 at Ravensbourne, winning 24-3. Before the start of a season, it was always recommended to get a Tetanus injection, particularly if some of the game fixtures were in London or Essex. This was, so I understood because many of the pitches had been laid over medieval plague pits. One club's ground we played on in the City of London, HAC - Honourable Artillery Company, (just a stone's throw from the old Whitbread brewery in Chiswell Street) was used as a burial site during the great plague in 1665.

A typical match day and game

Many of us worked on Saturday mornings (typically a 5½ day week in those days) we would often meet up for lunch prior to travelling to wherever the afternoon match was scheduled. The proto-type of the fast food restaurant chain, *Wimpy* (developed by J Lyons & Co., another 'house' rugby opponent) with their hallmark squeezy red-tomato sauce dispensers had appeared in the mid 1950's. However, a regular haunt for some of the team was a more singular traditional 'greasy spoon' known as the *Green Café* in Eccleston Street at the back of Victoria Station. We could get a good fry-up, sausage, bacon and egg, with bread and butter and a cup of tea for a modest cost of about 2/- (5p in new money). During the season, Charing Cross station around Saturday midday was often full of similar rugby players travelling to various suburban venues. Once changed into our playing kit, we would collectively place watches, wallets in the so called 'valuables box', at the home ground for safe keeping or alternatively at away matches given to a girl-friend supporter. Some of the rare action photographs of club matches (in this book) were actually taken by some of these stoic girl-friends (Liz, Rosie, et al). It was usual from time to time for a referee, (depending how conscientious he was) to visit our changing room before the match to make an inspection of our studs, usually as a response to directives from the Society of Referees, concerning injuries. The type of stud often used in boots then (cheapest) were made of leather fixed to the sole with four fine pins. After a while they would wear down leaving the pin-heads protruding, this could leave many opponents, with evidence of what Brian Moore, the ex-England hooker and television commentator would call 'a shoeing' after a ruck. The same checks would be made on cygnet or wedding rings and if they couldn't be taken off they had to be taped up, again to prevent injury. Some forwards wore leather 'scrum caps' - the norm then –no fancy coloured adhesive tape. Shin-pads were used if playing in the front row – and if not available I have seen a thick magazine (Readers' Digest) stuffed down the inside of socks work just as well. The front row would often defer shaving on a match day adding to 'their abrasive' aggression in the tight. The ball was heavier then, with six laces securing the inner bladder. It was made from four brown leather panels stitched together, eventually turning darker and loosing its shape.

'At half time oranges are not the only fruit –there are lemons too'! This was a war-time reference made by one of our opponents Great Western Railways (GWR -RFC), who recorded that at one match there were – 'No lemons, No bath, No tea, Plenty of beer'. The reference to lemons is interesting in that apparently they used to be the accepted half-time refresher at all rugger levels. The use of oranges was considered to be effete. Wartime conditions meant the end of the import of lemons (largely from Italy) and when available oranges were substituted. Interestingly there has been no subsequent return to lemons. A few would often 'light-up' for a quick smoke. One of the front row forwards (was it Rowley Hope?) was known to favour a swig from his hip-flask –must have made the second half scrums interesting! Typical rugby non-conformity emerged regularly on the pitch with the wearing of 'white shorts' as opposed to club navy blue. These included, Roy Butcher, Mike Lakin, Robin Garrett, Jim Collett, Jim Munnick, Pete Shaw and Harry Masterton-Smith, some players extended it to jerseys' and socks as well.

A rugby XV is made up more or less equally by forwards and backs and nowhere is the difference better explained than a comment made by Bill Beaumont a forward and one time England captain when he reflected, *'If I had been a winger, I might have been daydreaming and thinking about how to keep my kit clean for next week'*. This theme was fervently endorsed by one time Wallaby (Australian) forward and author Peter Fitzsimons when he commented, *'Rugby backs can be identified because they generally have clean jerseys and identifiable partings in their hair... come the revolution the backs will be the first to be lined up against the wall and shot for living parasitically off the work of others'*.

It was usually the responsibility of the team captain of the home side after the match on Saturday to telephone a newspaper bureau with the match results, for publishing in the Sunday Newspapers, like the *Times* and *Telegraph*. On a Sunday morning, there is something thrilling about reading your club's results in a newspaper –especially if you've won!

Unknown ground and opposition c.1957   (Photo Hugh Dalzell)
Cook's RFC *left to right*: ☺?, Don Keston (distance), Tony Gold
(scrum cap), Derek Sells (scrum cap), Gary Mos –being bundled into
touch

'Then there's fuddling about in the public-house,

*and drinking bad spirits and punch, and such rot-gut stuff. That won't
make drop-kicks or chargers of you, take my word for it.'*
Tom Brown's Schooldays', Chapter VI 'After the match'

Despite this earlier warning, Chris Laidlaw, the famous
All Black scrum-half concluded *'beer and rugby are
more or less synonymous'.* It could have been echoed
by many others. You only have to look at the
sponsorship names of today to see why. The English
clubs played (until 2010) in the *'Guinness'* premiership
and the European rugby competition is known as the
'Heineken' cup. And surprise, surprise, England Rugby
has *Greene King IPA a*s its official sponsor, whilst the
Welsh internationals had a Cardiff brewer *'Brains'*
emblazoned on their shirts. Not to be outdone the Irish
play in the *Magners* League, (an Irish cider made in
Tipperary, -yes, it really is a long way), and Scotland
has an official sponsorship deal with *Carling* –the beer,
that is, not the ex English Captain. The public house is

at the heart of the nation's social life, so it's not surprising that pubs play an integral part of the rugby game. As one commentator put it, *'The pub is as much a part of rugby as is the playing field,'* of course it is – stating the obvious. Quite apart from the after game refreshments, they were used as meeting places, before the game and sometimes as changing rooms as well. I recall playing an away match in Cheshunt against the *Old Cestrians* in 1959, where we changed in the *Green Dragon* pub (see photo) close to their ground. *Rosslyn Park* also used a pub, the *White Horse* in Hampstead

as a changing room in their first season. Other clubs such as the *Old Masonians* were formed in the *White Hart* at Hampton Wick in Surrey, close to their pitch in Home Park. The famous *Wasps FC* was formed at the *Eton & Middlesex Tavern* in North London. Slightly more up-market perhaps, the *Old Caterhamians* formed their club in the Edwardian *Bonnington Hotel* in London (now Park Inn) no doubt after an agreeable dinner. *The London Scottish Football Club* was founded in 1878 at *MacKay's Tavern* (where else), in Water Lane, Ludgate Hill, which was close to the old Thomas Cook's Chief Office at Ludgate Circus. The hugely successful *Hong Kong Sevens* was the result of 'Tokkie' Smith, Chairman of Hong Kong RFC and Ian Gow, a Rothman's Tobacco Company Executive chatting in the *'Bottom's Up'* club in Kowloon Hong Kong in 1974. (This bar featured in the James Bond film *'Man with the Golden Gun'* the same year). In 1868 the newly formed *Brighton FC,* (now the Brighton Blue's) had its administration headquarters in *Waters Wine Bar* at the bottom of Spring Street. It will therefore come as no surprise that the recruitment for the reconstituted

Cook's rugby section in 1953 was held at *The Goat Tavern* in Stafford Street (a short stroll from Berkeley Street).

Apart from booze, fags (cigarettes) were synonymous too, in fact most of us smoked, it was the social norm. The tobacco slogans *'You're never alone with a Strand'*, *'make mine a minor'*, and *'Waiter, twenty Guards please'*, *'today's cigarette is a Bristol'*, and (if really posh), *'do have a Du Maurier'* are easily recalled from advertisements of the time. Even in the mid 1970's the successful British Lions' captain Willie John McBride smoked a pipe, and as late as 1998 awarded 'pipe smoker of the year' by the British Pipesmokers' Council. When Cook's rugby club was revived in the early fifties, the price of a pint of beer was 1/3d, (5¼p) and nearly 60% of all men smoked. You could buy tipped cigarettes like *Benson & Hedges 'Olivier'* for 3/10 (about 19p) for twenty –or if feeling 'flush' *Wills Whiffs* a small cigar could be had for 3/11 for five. Ten years later the price of a pint had increased to 1/9d, (5¾p) and the number of men smoking slightly reduced by five percent, possibly helped by the newly introduced ban on television cigarette advertisements. *Senior Service* was a popular brand of cigarettes with club members (see photos). Like 'Pincher' Martin before me, I was a pipe-man, experimenting with *Balkan Sobranie*, (expensive) or the more usual (cheaper) Dutch tobacco, like *Van Rossems* Cavendish.

At that time, London had some fine brewers like *Fullers* in Chiswick, and *Young's* in Wandsworth, but it was *Watney's* Red Barrel, a 'keg' bitter which became really popular in the sixties and seventies. It was produced by the Stag Brewery in Pimlico, and became a cultural phenomenon of that era, when it was parodied in the Monty Python 'Travel Agent' sketch in 1969. Keg became a term of contempt by some, particularly in Britain, when pasteurised draught beers started replacing traditional cask beers. The quality of the process was not as good then as it is today, and sometimes the keg beers were referred to as plastic beer, largely because the chemicals used to create a foam or head on the finished beer. Despite this consumer concern, keg beer was replacing traditional cask ale in all parts of the UK, primarily because it requires less care to handle. Luckily for us all a group of beer-drinkers in the early 1970's formed the Campaign for Real Ale (CAMRA) because they had become fed up with the increasing bad quality of beer in Britain that was too fizzy, no character and no taste. Membership grew and today, with over 100,000 members it is one of the most successful consumer group in Europe, it promotes good-quality real ale and pubs, (we can all drink to that) as well as acting as the consumer's champion in relation to the beer and drinks industry. If CAMRA had not been formed to save real ale then this classic, great-tasting British drink would have become extinct; and it all started in Kruger's bar in Dunquin, Co Kerry Ireland, where else? Watney's along with its Red Barrel was consigned to history.

Clubhouse songs and pantomime performances
'Ik bin der Musikmeister,...Oh no he isn't...Oh yes he is!'

Typically many of the songs we sang were based on traditional folk songs like *'On Ilkla Moor baht 'at?! Wheear 'as ta bin sin ah saw thee,* ('*Where's that?'* a typical response if sung down south) hymns such as the Welsh *'Cwm Rhondda'* (The unofficial Welsh National Anthem), *'Guide me, O Thou great Jehovah, Pilgrim through this barren land'*, ending with, *'Feed me till I want no more'*, sung in close harmony. These and many popular ballads had been passed down over the years, with many adaptations over two world wars, and even more changes of lyrics with the passing of time and custom. Some were amusing and clever whilst many more were completely vulgar, and these usually sung as the evening progressed and beer took effect. Some of the lyrics and melodies were memorable – even to this day. Many teams we played against had some eloquent and entertaining raconteurs –as many had been in the forces where it was often customary in messes and wardrooms to sing for one's supper, -in other words entertain. We would sing together in the clubhouse bar with opponents and trade verse for verse. Nothing was written down as it was part of an oral tradition, it had to be memorised. It was particularly important to 'out sing' any opponents that we'd lost to as part compensation. The effect on the vocal chords of this strenuous amateur effort mixed with cigarettes or pipe tobacco would produce an extremely hoarse voice, several octaves lower – particularly on Sunday mornings, which found many of us repeating the mantra of the self-inflicted *never again*.

There is barely a rugby club in the land that doesn't have some players who will cross-dress for occasions without batting an eyelid, and without an inward look at their deeper motivation (for example some songs demand a female response). The English particularly have had a long and unique tradition of amateur female impersonation, dressing up in frocks, and wearing make-up passed down through Pantomime. Think Les Dawson, Dick Emery, the Two Ronnie's, and Danny La Rue, to Paul O'Grady (aka Lilly Savage), David Walliams and Matt Lucas. It seems a bizarrely and specifically British activity (you only have to glance at some the English supporters at the Six Nations Internationals or in festival mood at the Hong Kong Sevens); it's opaquely weird and embarrassing to the rest of the world. They are so at ease looking ridiculous, so accepting of the ridicule and the utter unsexiness of drag, that they are happily to accept its camp implications and enter into the high jinks with gusto. (Personally I admit to dressing as Marlene Dietrich singing (badly) *'Falling in love again...'* as part of an entertainment during a long Ashridge management training course). Even Lawrence Dellaglio the ex England International in his 2010 charity bike ride Rome to Edinburgh managed to dress up for at least one sector. In fact dressing up was also something of a Cook's tradition. The company archives have published photographs of the grandchildren of the company's founder, Frank and Bert Cook quite happily posing dressed up in Greek or Egyptian costume. (Bert was a wild young man with extravagant tastes and liked a drink or two, and by contrast Frank was shy and retiring). Some of the Cook's Amateur Operatic & Choral Society had of course been dressing up as girls since 1924, (albeit in a theatrical way) performing the *'Maid of the Mountains'* (1939), *'No No Nanette'* (1955) and *'Call me Madam'* (1958) to name just a few. In 1963 there was another 'dressing up' stunt, that of Miss Jemima Morrell's Swiss Tour, the brainchild of Bill Cormack our enterprising publicity manager at the time. It celebrated the centenary of Thomas Cook's first conducted alpine tour led by his great-great grandson and namesake. They all dressed up in Victorian dress, it was widely reported and as many as 20,000 people turned out when the party reached Interlaken.

'…all the…voices join in, not mindful of harmony,
but bent on noise, which they attain decidedly, but the general effect isn't bad.'   Tom Brown's Schooldays, Chapter VI 'After the match'

Some of the lyrics to rugby songs are completely unprintable, involving singing about such diverse subjects as: the *Sexual Life of a Camel*, the daughter of the *Major of Bayswater*, the story of *Eskimo Nell*, the court of *Old King Cole* and the exploits of the bold Russian, *Ivan Skavinsky Skavar*. Others included frequent requests for *Dinah, to show us your leg*, a yard above your knee, the *Wild West Show* including the *Oozelum bird* - who used to fly in ever decreasing circles, until it disappeared, et cetera, and of course the exploits of the good girls of *Roedean School*. London Scottish introduced us to the goings on at *The Ball of Kirriemuir*, and HMS President told us about the homecoming of *Barnacle Bill the Sailor* and alternative lyrics to the *Sailor's Hornpipe*. The colleges and the medical schools were good at parodying the song *'These Foolish Things'*, (a classic 1930's *'Mayfair song'* by Eric Maschwitz who was one time Head of Variety at the BBC). These lyrics, had endless verses (usually about diseases) ending with *'remind me of you'*. An example of the style (original & parody):

These Foolish Things (Remind me of you)

A cigarette that bears a lipstick's traces,
An airline ticket to romantic places,
Bought at Thomas Cook's too -
These foolish things, remind me of you.

That sofa bed we kissed and loved on,
Your mother's aspidistra we relieved ourselves on,
There'll be no blooms this spring -
These foolish things, remind me of you.

A tinkling piano in the next apartment,
Those stumblin' words that told you what my heart meant,
A fairground's faded swings -
These foolish things, remind me of you.

A cigarette that bears a Players label
A pint of Keg to put him under the table
He works at Thomas Cook's too -
These foolish things remind us of you.

The evergreen *'Marrying Kind'* would be sung most often, particularly at Old Boys clubhouses, as the repetitive words are easy to remember. The verses go through the various rugby positions as follows. (The lyrics of this song sung by male players seem curiously from a woman's point of view).

If I were the Marrying Kind, Sir

If I were the marrying kind,
Which thank the lord I'm not sir?
The kind of man that I would wed,
Would be a rugby full-back.
He'd find touch,

and I'd find touch,
We'd both find touch together.
We'd be alright in the middle of the night,
Finding touch together.

Repeat, (through various playing positions, et cetera)

For the 'camp style' performer, the following popular clubhouse song, invites a response from the other team, with the combined teams joining in the chorus. It was sung to the tune of the *'Eton Boating Song'*. There are endless verses depending on the creative Limerick ability of singers; here are a couple of verses.

We're all Queers Together

My name is Cecil, and I live in Berkeley Square,
I wear skin-tight trousers and ribbons in my hair,

Chorus:
For we're all queers together,
That's why we go around in pairs,
Yes we're all queers together,
Now excuse us while we go upstairs.

I went for a ride on a tube-train,
it was crowded; I had to stand,
A little boy offered me his seat, so I squeezed it with my hand,

For we're all queers together,
That's why we go around in pairs,
Yes we're all queers together,
Now excuse us while we go upstairs.

All this of course was an earlier age far away from political correctness, and before taking down your trousers in public became unacceptable. But in rugby circles as the French say, *'plus ça change, plus c'est la même chose'*. The more things change (apparently), the more they remain the same (in fact).

After game entertainments

The 1960's - for some, marked the end for 'Victorian values' and the beginning of the permissive society. It was a time of freedom, a decade of social unrest, innocence lost, scandal, war, sex, drugs and rock and roll. However, if we did not always obey the rules, at that time we knew what they were. It is often said in the smug and self regarding Woodstock version that anyone who can remember the sixties –wasn't really there, but of course we were. Sometimes the passing of time only allows memory the occasional glimpse of past events. Later in the same decade Philip Larkin's reflective poem *'Annus Mirabilis',* (year of wonders), spoke for many.

> *Sexual intercourse began*
> *In nineteen sixty-three*
> *(Which was rather late for me)-*
> *Between the end of the Chatterley ban*
> *And the Beatles' first LP.*

Our casual dress in the 1950's and early 1960's was to wear a sports jacket, blazer or perhaps a hand-knitted pullover (thanks mum) with tie and slacks. (see photos). Harry Masterton-Smith, reflecting forty-years on, remarks *'...and I can't get over our post match dress code! There's a meaningful social comment in there somewhere!* It was of course very much what our fathers and uncles wore in the thirties and forties. War-time clothes rationing had only ended five years before the club was revived, and choice was limited. What probably immediately stands out when perusing photos of the period are the clothes and haircuts? Winter coats (often war-surplus duffel-coats), occasional fair-isle pullovers and striped college style scarves. Think *'Lucky Jim'* (Ian Carmichael as Jim Dixon' in the 1957 film of the Kingsley Amis novel) or 'Burberry style' raincoats (folded over the arm) were the norm – relaxed designer sports wear and stylish 'outdoor' clothing had yet to make its mark. But

Carnaby Street fashion was about to change all that (well for the girls anyway).

Clubhouse drinking games would be part and parcel of the game. Harry recalls *'we had a successful 'Boat Race' team – two of us anchored it with four second pints'*. Usually, during the evening a challenge would be made to the opponents, with one of the team starting singing *'Can you play the muffin-man'* (at the same time attempting to balancing a full pint beer mug on the top of his head- without spilling it), *the muffin man, the muffin man, Can you play the muffin man who lives down Drury Lane'*, response *'Yes I can play the muffin man'*, *et cetera* (responding to the challenge also placing a beer mug on head) –it didn't last long as most were drenched in beer, what a waste!

On occasion usually after a home game, if the visitors, or entertainment and carousing had petered out, we'd decide to go up to town. An assorted group would take the train from Ravensbourne to London. On these occasions we'd enjoy ourselves either by singing a few songs to entertain fellow passengers (most of which pretended it wasn't happening) or if it was quiet play the *'poster game'*. Now the poster game was an extreme sport as it required both dexterity and split-second timing. It involved slipping out of the train at a station, selecting a suitable poster (usually a film), tearing it off, and quickly returning to the train before it moved off again. There was a knack to this, being easier than first thought. The trick was to lift the bottom edge corner pulling steadily upwards and because of the paste used –the poster usually came away quickly and cleanly. These posters would be rolled up very quickly before re-entering the train (door kept open). These trophies became part of a personal collection or if damaged given to a (surprised) ticket collector at the end of journey. Bobbie Gould became quite adept at this 'extreme sport' but some of the novices were occasionally left literally on the platform, waiting for the next train. On one occasion we introduced the game to our Dutch visitors from Hilversum, who thought it great fun, providing some authentic (and original) English souvenirs.

It had to be Soho

Once in London we would head for Soho – perhaps Luigi's or a Chinese meal in Chinatown possibly followed by Ronnie Scott's Jazz Club, (depending on cash reserves) which had opened in a basement in Gerrard Street in 1959. Roy Bannister recalls a little Jazz cellar off the Charing Cross road where huge plate-fulls of Spaghetti Bolognaise and beers were served. This was a regular haunt of the First XV in the  1950's often including many opposition players too. There was always a buzz in Soho late into the evening, and was the centre of Jazz and coffee bars, not to mention pubs and low life. But the old post war bohemian spirit of Soho was disappearing. The Fifties Soho with coffee bars like the *Heaven & Hell* and the *2i's* were the birthplace of British *rock' n' roll* and the home of *skiffle*. Cliff and the boys were associated with the *2i's* Coffee Bar in Old Compton Street, and the nearby *Moka Coffee Bar* in Frith Street (first to have a Gaggia expresso coffee machine), just a short distance from the music publishers.  In the early sixties the scene changed and was pretty much wiped out by the '*Beatles*' and the '*Stones*'.

Most Cook's team players worked in London, so apart from weekends –some of us knew it well from week-day business. I was still a lowly travel clerk, so to supplement my meagre salary and rugby expenses I used to moonlight in the evenings. Firstly, back stage (props) at Her Majesty's Theatre in the Haymarket. (I even had to join the NATKI union). The show running at the time –was the American Musical *'Bye Bye Birdie'* with Chita Rivera and Marty Wilde. One evening I was chatting with him in the wings whilst waiting for his on-stage cue, he asked me what University I was going to. Confused, I replied *'none, I'm working, why'*? His enquiry had been because I *'spoke proper'*. (This *'speaking proper'* habit once earnt me a punch in the back of the head q.v. *Old Ignatians*). I progressed to a bar-man in Soho –it paid better, and got to know the area and some characters well. My first pub was the *Blue Post* in Rupert Street, more a cocktail bar really, along a passageway from *Ronnie Scott's* in Gerard Street where Georgie Fame was performing at the time. I moved on to the *Coach & Horses* in Greek Street,

working for Norman Balon, who by his own admission was the rudest Landlord in London. He was tall, dark with rounded shoulders, always wore a suit and was a passable look-a-like for the actor Walter Matthau. His catchphrase *'You're barred, you Bastard'*, alternated with the more conventional *'get out and stay out'*. He once allegedly barred his own mother *('she's bloody past it')*. Whilst many found him difficult and moody (especially tourists), I found him a good evening employer. If it was quiet, rather than stand polishing glasses, I'd offer to wash his Austin 1800 car, parked nearby for an extra ten bob (50p in new money). Sometimes after closing time, he'd drop me off at Baker Street Tube station as we both lived in North London. In the evening session, Norman would only let 'selected' people (the regulars) have food, and I'd be detailed to make them toasted cheese and ham sandwiches. Another regular was the was ubiquitous Jeffrey Bernard, the louche gambler, writer, drinker of ill repute, and *The Spectator's* Low Life columnist, (his life at the *Coach and Horses* was later made into a Keith Waterhouse stage play *'Jeffrey Bernard is unwell'*, played by Irish actor Peter O'Toole). The pub also became a meeting place for the editorial staff of *'Private Eye'*, with the likes of editor Richard Ingrams, and cartoonist Willie Rushton. The pub later featured the magazine's brilliant strip cartoon *'The Regulars'*, drawn by Michael Heath. Round the corner the Palace theatre was showing the *Sound of Music* and during the course of the run we had many of the cast actors and actresses regularly dropping in for a drink. On one occasion in the early sixties I served a 'Nun in Costume' (outside the theatre this is strictly against the rules) defiantly smoking a pipe and enjoying a pint at the bar!

The pubs were numerous but one that is memorable (from personal experience) is the old *York Minster*, in Dean Street, known then -and now officially as the *French House* with its stylish, cheque-cashing (if he liked you) landlord Gaston Berlemont, who sported a French handle-bar moustache. An early wine bar with a lingering smell of Gauloise, they refused to sell beer in pint glasses –even today. Once the haunt of Dylan Thomas, Francis Bacon and later the larger than life artist and writer Sandy Fawkes, a close friend of Daniel Farson, the television journalist, chronicler of Soho and spectacular drunk. She made fashion drawings for *Vanity Fair* and the *Daily Sketch*, becoming their fashion editor until the early 1970's. Married to Wally Fawkes, a clarinettist (used to play at *Ronnie Scott's*) and celebrated *Daily Mail* cartoonist with his strip *Flook*. They lived in Hampstead and their house was known for its lively parties. There were many clubs, such as *Murray's Cabaret* and the *Pinstripe Club*, in

Kingly Court. This is where Christine Keeler met John Profumo and it also hosted revellers such as Oliver Reed and Peter O'Toole. Soho also had many seedy drinking clubs, because before 1988, pubs closed at 3pm. So committed drinkers adjourned to afternoon drinking clubs (and in the travel business many airline reps entertained and led us astray). One of these off the Charing Cross Road was a leprous cellar, with rising damp forcing its way through the plaster, called the *Kismet Club,* popular with actors. Its nicknames included *'The Iron Lung'* and *'Death in the Afternoon'.* On one occasion a passing visitor asked what the strange smell was there. *'Failure,'* came the limp reply. Another was the *Colony Club Room,* (often called Muriel's after the owner) in Dean Street, opened after the war by Muriel Belcher, a combative, foul-mouthed but enterprising lesbian, who with her Jamaican squeeze Carmel, created a meeting place for writers, painters like Francis Bacon and amusing hard drinkers. Muriel developed a cult of rudeness –telling anyone she thought boring to eff-off. The room upstairs was a small place, decorated in industrial green. Customers at its little bar wallowed in the agreeable air of seediness, their imbibing overlooked by sometimes fine works of art donated by the insolvent artists in settlement of bar bills. It became the scene of decades of bad behaviour, involving some of the best names in the business. Dylan Thomas threw up there, Tom Driberg propositioned there and Jeffrey Bernard advanced towards literal leglessness in its smoky confines. She ran it till her death in 1979.

What made (some of) us laugh?

The early sixties was a time when the establishment was being challenged, old ways, pomposity and hypocrisy satirised. *The Footlights* had produced many talents that was to make lasting impact on the times and society. The satirical magazine *Private Eye* had been launched in 1961 with editor Richard Ingrams.

The financial help came from the brilliant Peter Cook who in turn created the *Establishment Club* in Soho, the forerunner of many comedy clubs. This sweaty, smoky club was packed to capacity every night and offered punters the chance to see the latest talents to rise from Oxford and Cambridge, along with acts from America such as the notorious Lenny Bruce, (despite his critically acclaimed run in 1962, was subsequently refused re-entry to the UK). There was a film which became a bit of a cult, screened in London in 1960, which we would often see over and over again. It was a short (only 11 minutes) with Spike Milligan known as the *'Running, Jumping & Standing Still'* film. We (well some of us) also enjoyed the records of the decidedly 'sinister' alternative comedian Ivor Cutler with his humorous monologues. He was appearing on the stage at the Comedy theatre in *'An Evening of British Rubbish'* at this time. Then in 1963 we had the Profumo affair –a gift to the comedians and satirists. This provided a host of characters from Christine Keeler, the Russian Eugene Ivanov, a Soviet naval attaché, Mandy Rice-Davies (her response, -which became a catchphrase, *'He would wouldn't he'* - when in court she was told that Lord Astor disputed her recollection of events) and of course Jack Profumo himself –a cabinet minister. A record made at the time -a spoof sketch with Anthony Newley and his (then) wife Joan Collins; acted out the love triangle in a series of voice-overs on a recording called *'Fool Britannia'.* This provided us with many sketches to mimic (Bobbie Gould had obtained a copy from Dobell's where his older brother worked). BBC TV's *'That Was The Week That Was',* also became compulsive late evening viewing - with David Frost making his name, it regularly achieved millions viewers.

The parties

Throughout the season there were always weekend parties. A popular entrance fee was the 'Party Four' named after the keg beer that could be purchased in

tins containing four pints or later Party Seven (seven pints). Brewed by the ubiquitous Watneys of Red Barrel fame – but when you are young you simply haven't developed a drinker's palate! By early 1963 I shared a small flat in Pimlico, and by now an old school chum had arrived from Wales studying medicine (and nurses) at the Royal Free hospital. It seemed particularly if you were single, life was one long party.

As Wordsworth wrote a century before about another social revolution, *'Bliss was it in that dawn to be alive, but to be young was very heaven!'*

As Harry recalls *'I remember all night parties in Tooting which were mainly an extended 'drinkfest' to which we all brought something to consume and chipped in for a barrel of beer. Also kipping on the floor in a house round the corner from the Warwick Arms in Earls Court, and being woken with a slobbery kiss by the host's boxer dog. It did save having to walk all the way home to Harrow'*. These 'drinkfests' were held in Hugh Dalzell's South London flat and well attended by many first XV players like Mike Lidbetter, Bob Maidment and Brian Wright.

Some of the alternative parties for the 'A' XV were held in the home of Steve Sutcliffe-Hey, a house he shared with his brother in Sutton. They were as different as chalk is from cheese, Steve the extrovert, his brother the introvert. He had returned to England after serving in the Far East as a Merchant Navy deck officer. Steve had worked for a shipping line serving Hong Kong and Yokohama in Japan on a regular cargo service. Assuming the monotony of this journey, he apparently had acquired two wives, one at each end. We used to ask him, how this bigamous arrangement worked, only to be told *'they never meet each other'* with a mischievous grin. However, he had returned to the UK without them. Our party entertainment apart from drinking was to listen to humorous records of comedians like Peter Sellers and Spike Milligan. Peter Sellers had made many records full of comedy sketches many of which we could repeat word for word whilst listening to the LP's. One of these sketches involving a BBC presenter interviewing the Irish playwright and infamous drunk Brendan Behan. Derek Sells was particularly good at mimicking his accent and re-enacting his notorious television interview with, *'Could I not sink a couple of drinks right now'* pause, then said with urgency and menacingly louder emphasis *'a couple at this very minute'...* would have us in fits of laughter. We found some Noël Coward records hugely amusing –but this sort of 'art deco age' of sophisticated entertainment was rapidly drifting out of fashion. However, his command of language, rhythm and rhyme not to mention an ear for a catchy melody became a great source of entertainment to us. The first line of the song, *'Someday I'll find you'* would usually be parodied with -'creep up behind you', or in his *'Alice is at it again'*, would receive a riposte whilst nudging a fellow player saying, 'he's singing about your sister' - and so on. We enjoyed his stories of *'Uncle Harry'* -'he's not a missionary now –he's left the island' and *'A Bar on the Piccola Marina'* (the story of the liberated Mrs Wentworth-Brewster in Capri). After repetitive playing, we could easily sing along with Noël, and 'camp it up' ourselves. These quite harmless 'high jinks' were not quite enjoyed as much by Steve's brother. Partly because of his shyness or lack of humour (he didn't drink much) - we teased him mercilessly about his clothes and choice of pullovers. Singing remarks about his appearance such as; *'Funny little fellow, wear's his sister's clothes, don't know what to call him but I think he's one of those'*. And to make things worse, we used to teasingly squeeze his bum, jokingly on the way to the lavatory, usually singing –*'excuse us while we go upstairs'* He was quite convinced after a few parties, that many (all) of us were gay –so his brother gleefully reported afterwards! 'We all found this hilarious (as did his brother) – the thoughtlessness of youth when partying! As the evening wore on - in no state to reach the railway station – even if there was a train at two in the morning, we stayed over crashing out wherever there was space. These high jinks came to a head, with an apparent serious disagreement between the 'brothers Sutcliffe-Hey', which resulted in our Sutton entertainments coming to an end.

There were other parties of course –one being held by Mike Lakin and his wife Sheila at their house in Kenton. This was during the 1964/5 season when he was Captain of the First team. However this party was more 'grown up' as girl friends were invited so the singing was kept to the clean minimum, but despite that it went on into the early hours much to the distress of his neighbours.

Club dinners and the closed season

After the winter season's games finished some of us (the single ones –without girl friends) were often at a loss what to with ourselves during summer weekends and to keep in touch with club mates. Ravensbourne was an all year sports ground, with summer facilities for cricket and lawn tennis. The cricket section was well subscribed so getting a game was difficult – although established players like Hugh Dalzell managed to play, as did Pete Simmonds and 'Pincher' Martin. The section was under the fanatical leadership of Andy Anderson, who used to schedule as many games as possible at Ravensbourne, as the pitch was considered one the best in the South East. There were some excellent grass tennis courts and Roy Bannister played for the club in the men's double team. I used to enjoy the odd game of tennis too, sometimes with Steve Sutcliffe-Hey, -usually losing, but not many others played. Roy Butcher enjoyed his summer weekend leisure idly at home getting under his parents feet, and recalls his father eagerly looking forward to the opening of the next rugby season.

There has been a long tradition in rugby club circles to hold an end of season formal club dinner or supper. It usually involved a compliant hotel or pub room, a guest of honour, a company director, departmental heads or perhaps a 'big' name or legend in the game. Eventually they developed into a raucous evening involving throwing bread rolls (usually soaked in bitter) and getting banned from the venue selected.

In August 1926 there is a record of an end of season dinner for the *Ludgate Circus XV* (as the club was known then) at the Grafton Hotel. Built in the new Edwardian British Colonial' style in 1903 'located in Tottenham Court Road, (now part of Radisson Edwardian Group). This dinner appears to have become an annual event. On that occasion it was voted the most exhilarating and enjoyable evening ever spent by the sections members. It had become a 'section' custom to award 'Honour Caps' to outstanding players during the season. On this occasion two players had

Grafton Hotel, Tottenham Court Road, London

awards R. Coussens (Forward) and E.J.K. Higgins (Right Centre), *'who received hearty congratulations from all present'*. It was in the same Tottenham Court Road that around seventy years earlier two hooligans –

whilst on an evening out on what they called a 'beer trip', smashed four or five street gas lamps for fun in the early hours of the morning. They only managed to escape the police by slipping down a side street. Their names were Karl Marx and Frederick Engels.

One of our opponents clubs GWR, recalls, that they would regularly hold their dinners at the Great Western Hotel in Paddington, and in the season 1927/8 the guest of honour was the legendary rugby player and England International *Wavell Wakefield* (providing him with their club's 'Honours Cap'). It eventually became a wild evening, particularly after about 9 pm down in the Refreshment Room on No 1 Platform. In the light of this experience the first priority guest at subsequent Dinners was the Chief of the GWR transport police.

Unfortunately, by the time the post war Thos. Cook & Son's RFC had been re-established in 1953 – this tradition along with the 'Honours Cap' awards was never revived. Shame!

9. Final no side

'.....And it's not for the sake of a ribboned coat,
Or the selfish hope of a season's fame,
but his Captain's hand on his shoulder smote,
Play up! play up! and play the game.'
Henry Newbolt's *'Vitaï Lampada'* written in 1897

The referee has blown his whistle. So now dear reader having travelled this far you will have learnt something about the spirit and bonhomie of the amateur game, shared the memories of a few Cook 'house' players. As one of them, Harry Masterton-Smith recalled with affection, *'At any one time, it seems there were more Old Boys than Cook's employees in the (house) teams, which is testament to how much we enjoyed our time together both on and off the pitch'*. His sentiments were echoed by many others, Hugh Dalzell remembers negotiating 'associate' club membership for some non –Thomas Cook players, to ensure they had a game.

You will have read about the fun we enjoyed, and the amazing range of opposition teams we played in an amateur rugby era over forty years ago; all whilst working for *the* great travel company, (where it was *de rigeuer* to arrive and leave head office wearing a trilby in the 1930's) and its sports club that brought us all together. You now know what the ninety-nine signal meant, what the Jesuits did with a ferula, the cost of a pint and packet of cigarettes in old money and why 'real' men have oval balls. Travelling with us on tour to Holland you might have marvelled how an amateur XV could have become TV celebrities overnight. Whilst further reflecting on RC Hilversum 'macho' website message *'if you like action and can take a beating'* then, that might be the club for you. At least you will have learnt how to say thank you in Dutch. Certainly this was a 'different' type of Cook's tour. Although you are still probably none the wiser about the difference between a ruck and a maul – then neither were we playing the game. As Jonathan Davies (described as the last great Welsh fly-half) once a panellist on BBC

TV's 'A Question of Sport' responded, *'I think you enjoy the game more if you don't know the rules. Anyway, you're on the same wavelength as the referees.* Having arrived at the final no side, it's time to kick the story into touch (sorry for the cliché's –they became irresistible). Let's make for the bar and that well deserved quiet pint, or perhaps as Gareth Chilcott the retiring Bath player put it after his last game, '...*followed by 17 noisy ones*'.

I had joined the club straight from school and still retained a schoolboy habit of keeping a diary. This is a summary of reflections during my first season 1959/60.

"We meet in Wembley on September 12th for a trial match. I play for the 'A' team against LMS 'A' at their home ground, we won by a large margin 41-3. The team atmosphere is buoyant, but the following four Saturday matches were lost, against Southern Railway Ex. 'A', (played scrum half), Wimbledon 'A', (scrum half then wing forward), Westminster Bank (my first match playing for the first XV) and London Scottish 'C' (played hooker) at the Richmond Athletic ground, there was much singing about a Ball in Kirriemuir. In late October, we enjoy success again, and more importantly my 'first try' in club rugby, playing centre, against the BBC 'A' team, at their splendid ground at Motspur Park (they have a spectacular row of individual bath-tubs adjacent to the changing rooms), we won 14-0. I got drunk. I am enjoying my rugby.

The New Year, late January 1960, I scored my 'second try' against Rochester Ex. 'A' we won 13-8 at Ravensbourne. We lost more than we won in the games that followed. In one of them after a heavy tackle I experienced my first dose of 'concussion' playing against Shirley Wanderers. It was curious and confusing sensation (in my 'foggy' state I hadn't a clue in which direction I should be attacking). In late February I am picked to play for the first team again, this time against the Standard Bank of South Africa, an away match on their home ground in Beckenham. I scored my third try of the season –it was converted so we won the match 5-0, much celebration and congratulations from Hugh Dalzell, (…'his Captain's hand on his shoulder smote'). I return (down to earth) to the 'A' team where we seem to have more fun, ending the season with wins against Barclays Bank and Woolwich Poly Ex. 'A'. In April, I'm selected to play in the Easter tour to Holland (flying to Amsterdam) playing wing forward against Hilversum –a match we won 13–9. Isn't life grand"?

After a motor cycle accident (knocked off an Italian scooter by a French car) in the early spring of 1965 my rugby playing days came to an abrupt end for the rest of that season. I did slowly recover and managed the odd game of cricket years afterwards but no rugby. Events and other responsibilities took precedent. So, did I miss playing the game? In his autobiography Bill McLaren explains his feelings after giving up match commentating after many years, as an experience similar to that of an addict going 'cold turkey'. Even today forty years on watching an international my reflexes occasionally twitch as if still playing.

A winter's tale

Imagine the scene if you will. It's a winter's Saturday afternoon, the sound of voices – it's the buzz of good natured banter from a crowded changing room. You are part of the team, tying up the final lace knot on your boots, catching that familiar smell of leather and Dubbin. Then filing out (with perhaps a friendly pat for *Brigitte*), along the corridor echoing to the clatter of many studs, with team mates to the pitch. The anticipation of a new game –running up and down on the spot and the 'butterflies' before 'kick-off', getting your tackle in first (memories of *'scythe them down'*). Taking a hit, releasing a team-mate to carry the ball, or the sheer joy of receiving and holding a pass -beating your man and running towards the line, ball in hands (there is no greater exhilaration known to man). The welcome half-time oranges, (perhaps a 'snifter' or smoke for the non-conformists) a group huddle, the captain's view of the game and individual performances so far (expletives deleted). Instinctively standing in line sportingly clapping our visitors - win or lose, into the Ravensbourne clubhouse with a friendly pat or two. At an away match receiving applause in turn (slightly embarrassed) from opponents on their home ground. Their hospitality too, occasionally providing half-pints of shandies, waiting for us in the changing room, to be gratefully downed in one, (with a theatrical belch from some). Staring vacantly at the floor strewn with clots of studded earth, sitting exhausted, on the benches under a row of hooks on which limply hangs an assortment of our togs. Wincing at some yet undiscovered injury and sensing the lingering medicated smell of wintergreen. The shaking hands and limited speech from physical effort followed by the examinations of a swollen lip or cut eye. Someone pulls out a packet of 'gaspers', reaching out for a (cadged) Players cigarette enjoying long pulls and exhaling at leisure. The steaming shirts heaped on the changing room floor, the shouts from the showers (especially if lukewarm or cold) and the bliss of jumping naked into a steaming hot plunge bath. Afterwards, freshly scrubbed (with the lingering scent of Wright's coal tar soap), into the bar. Glass mug in hand (held by the bowl-never the handle) anticipating the contents of the enamel beer jug, as it moves methodically on its pilgrimage around the team towards you. Marvelling and watching the sexy young girls the opposition clubhouses seemed to attract. The songs (learning new verses), social camaraderie, the sense of belonging, and the exquisite thought that this experience will repeat itself all over again –next Saturday.

And perhaps you still cannot fathom why boys and men do this, then, your answer is, as the French rugby enthusiast Pierre de Coubertin, said, *'In order to understand and appreciate it fully, one must have played it...this beautiful sport.'*

10. Fifty-seven old farts and other quotes...

Rugby has prompted many people to 'take a view' on the game or make astute observations. They range from PG Wodehouse and Peter Cook to Will Carling and Elizabeth Taylor; they've all had something different to say about the game.

"Rugby football is a game I can't claim absolutely to understand in all its niceties, if you know what I mean. I can follow the broad, general principles, of course. I mean to say, I know that the main scheme is to work the ball down the field somehow and deposit it over the line at the other end and that, in order to squelch this programme, each side is allowed to put in a certain amount of assault and battery and do things to its fellow man which, if done elsewhere, would result in 14 days without the option, coupled with some strong remarks from the Bench." P.G. Wodehouse, 'Very Good, Jeeves' (1930)

"The whole point of rugby is that it is, first and foremost, a state of mind, a spirit." Jean-Pierre Rives (1952-), former French rugby captain, who epitomised the Corinthian spirit and courage of the game, known as *Casque d'or* because of his long blond hair.

To Princess Anne's son Peter Phillips, Gordonstoun School's rugby captain, for his pre-match coin-toss preference: *"Grandmother or tails, sir?"* Anon. rugby referee (1995)

"Rugby is a game for the mentally deficient... That is why it was invented by the British. Who else but an Englishman could invent an oval ball?" Peter Cook, 'Beyond the Fringe' satirist, (1937-1995), who was made to play the game at Radley College.

"The first half is invariably much longer than the second. This is partly because of the late kick-off but is also

caused by the unfitness of the referee." Michael Green, *'The Art of Coarse Rugby'* (1960)

"The relationship between the Welsh and the English is based on trust and understanding. They don't trust us and we don't understand them." Dudley Wood, RFU Administrator, (1986)

"The lads say my bum is the equivalent of one 'Erica'." Bill Beaumont, England Captain 1978-1982. (Erica Roe was the busty girl who caused a stir by running topless onto the Twickenham pitch during England v Australia in 1982, a match which England won 15-11)

"If the game is run properly as a professional game, you do not need 57 old farts running rugby." Will Carling (1995), England's youngest ever Captain, whose remarks caused him to be sacked as Captain – but later re-instated after a public outcry.

"I prefer rugby to soccer. I enjoy the violence in rugby, except when they start biting each other's ears off." Elizabeth Taylor, (1972) film actress, (at the time married to Richard Burton, actor and Welsh rugby enthusiast)

"I would rather have played for Wales at the Arm's Park, than Hamlet at the Old Vic". Richard Burton, Welsh film and theatre actor (1925-1984)

"The women sit, getting colder and colder, on a seat getting harder and harder, watching oafs, getting muddier and muddier." - Virginia Graham, US writer and commentator, (1913-1998) referring to the 'muddied oafs' image conjured up by Rudyard Kipling in his poem 'The Islanders' (1902)

"When in doubt – kick it out" Derek Sells advice to new players, as Captain of the Cook's 'A' XV 1961-63

Reference Sources

The Thomas Cook Archive provided a wealth of reference material particularly old staff magazine articles and some photographs (as indicated). Paul Smith, Company Archivist, Thomas Cook UK & Ireland, Part of Thomas Cook Group plc, The Thomas Cook Business Park, Coningsby Road, Peterborough, PE3 8SB

www.thomascook.com

Bibliography:

Thomas Cook, 150 years of Popular Tourism, Piers Brendon, Seeker & Warburg, London, 1992, - *the best informative read on Thomas Cook, a must for anyone interested in travel and social history of this fascinating iconic company. It should be 'compulsory' for all company staff.*

Cook's Tours, The Story of Popular Travel, Edmund Swinglehurst, Blandford Press, Dorset, 1982, *a nostalgic visual feast for all travel affectionardo's.*

A Century in Photographs –Travel 1900-2000, Ian Harrison, Times Books/HarperCollins, London, 2000, *-a fascinating glimpse into the development of mass travel in the 20th century, the greatest liberation in history.*

The Union Game, A Rugby History, Sean Smith, BBC Worldwide Ltd., London, 1999, - *a comprehensive and excellent record of the BBC Television Series (same year), written with a Welsh passion for the game.*

World Rugby, Mark Ryan, Flame Tree Publishing, London, 2007, - *an excellent easy-to-use reference packed with information on world-wide rugby and players both union and league, written by a sports journalist and rugby enthusiast.*

Talking of Rugby, An Autobiography, Bill McLaren, Hutchinson, London, 1991, - *they don't make them like that any more - a much missed rugby commentator.*

Muddied Oafs, The soul of rugby, Richard Beard, Yellow Jersey Press, London, 2004, - *written by a player searching for the meaning of the game.*

The Art of Course Rugby, Michael Green, originally published in 1960, new edition in paperback 1995, Robson Books, London, – *an amusing book, written in the era many of us were playing, so close to the 'real' truth of the time.*

The Playfair Rugby Football Annual for 1962/3, Ed. O L Owen, published Dickens Press (Daily News), London, -*known as the 'Wisden' of rugby records, players and club information, published between 1948-1972.*

Tom Brown's Schooldays, Thomas Hughes, first published in 1856, Wordsworth Classics, Sixth Edition, Ware, Herts. 1993, - *still a good read.*

You're Barred, You Bastards! The Memoir of a Soho Publican, Norman Balon with Spencer Bright, Sidgwick & Jackson, London, 1991, -*a reminder of pub life and Soho characters in the sixties.*

Many web sites have been consulted. The following have been useful.

www.cantrugby.co.uk/clubs
- Steve Uglow of Canterbury RFC has created a very useful site listing all 1200 + English rugby union clubs playing in leagues, with helpful club links

www.Ovalballs.com
– run by John Hood a rugby enthusiast, (and self confessed anorak) where I was lucky enough to purchase some old Cook's rugby photographs and fixture memorabilia, excellent links to many other sites, particularly all things rugby

www.rugbyclubhilversum.nl
- this leading Dutch club has thoughtfully translated it's site into English (some of it literally) at a click of a button, they still welcome touring rugby clubs

www.RugbyData.com
– complete statistical analysis of worldwide international rugby records

www.Rugbyfootballhistory.com
- Nigel Trueman's comprehensive and interesting site on all things rugby

www.RFU.com
- HQ's excellent and informative site, including the world rugby museum

www.Sports-quotes.com
- an excellent site for many sporting quotes including rugby

www.timesonline.co.uk
archive article from Sunday Times, May 31 2009, titled 'The Lion that Roared' –an interview with Cliff Morgan by sports writer David Walsh

Appendix 1: TCRFC club players & officials 1953 – 1966

Whilst there are over sixty names, this list is not exhaustive, inevitably a few players from some team photographs cannot unfortunately be identified with a name. Note: Some of Thomas Cook's Berkeley Street departmental names were abbreviated, as follows: CTD – Conducted Tours Dept., FE –Foreign Exchange Dept., HTD –Holiday Tours Dept., IIT – Independent Inclusive Tours Dept., POD –Post Order Dept., others are probably self explanatory.

Player Name	known as	Dept/Office	Position, comments
Ashby, W	Bill?	?	(Forward) Hilversum visitors '59,
Bannister, R	Roy	Harrods & others	(Forward), founder member '53, Hilversum tour '58, retired '*injured*' '60,
Barrowman, R	Ron/Jock	FE	Hilversum tour '58, left company for a sales role in the Steel Industry,
Bascombe, D	Derek	POD ext 509	(Hon Sec. & Referee) for many years, Hilversum tours '58 & '60, as referee,
Bazzali, R	Romeo	Forwarding House	(Full back), Hilversum tours '58 and '60, 1st & A XV's
Block, G	Graham	HTD	7 a-side Dept team winners '58
Briddock, W	Bill	-	(Forward), Hilversum tour '60, (tour only)
Brooks, G	Geoff	POD	(Forward), 'A' team, '60/2 season Vice Capt 'A' XV '61/2,
Bulmer-Jones, V	Vic	Passports	(Forward), Ex RAF played 'A' team '60/64 visited Egypt in mid '70's, met Harry M-S, died 2009?
Butcher, R	Roy	FE	(Forward), First & 'A' team, '60/5, later played for *Dover RFC*,
Carter, J	John	Leadenhall St.	(Scrum half) Hilversum tour '58, ex Public school ? player, 7-a-side team '58
Collett, J	Jim	?	Season '60/1 'A' team
Dalzell, H A	Hugh	HTD ext 315, 749, 563	(Fly-half) Hilversum tours ''58 & '60, Hon. Match Sec., 1st XV Club Capt '59/61, V.Capt.'61/2, -his brother Richard occasionally played for TC

Player Name	known as	Dept/Office	Position, comments
Dangerfield, R	Roy	?	Capt '53/4, founder member,
Dann, R J	John	Pall Mall & others	(Scrum half/wing forward), played '59-'65, Hilversum tour '60, visitors '61 & '64
Davies, B	Brian	HTD	(Wing), Hilversum tours '58 and '60, 1st team player, 7-a-side team '58,
Davies, G	George	?	(Full Back) Hilversum tour '60, preferred soccer,
Davies, P	Pete	Coding	(Forward), Hilversum tour '58, 'A' team player '60/3
Dawson, P	Pete	London Office?	(Wing) *'a great tackler'*, 7-a-side runners up team '58
Dewdney, B	Brian	-	(Forward), Hilversum tour '60, (tour only)
Dowling, D	Dave	FE / Relief HTD	Believed to have died 1970's?, his cousin (Old Cryptians) played occasionally,
Down, A	Alex	? ext 479	Section secretary '53/4, founder member,
Garrett, R	Robin	Traffic Management 5th floor ext 350	(Full back/wing), seasons '60-4 'A' team, Hon. Team Sec. '64/5, Hilversum tours '63, & '65?
Gillies, P	?	?	(Wing) Hilversum visitors '59
Golds, A	Tony	I.I.T	Hilversum tour '58, & visitors '59
Gould, R	Bobby	?	(Wing), 'A' team player '60/3, retired injured '63? His elder brother played for TC occasionally
Halliday, G	George	FE	Had a *'Jimmy Edwards'* style handle-bar moustache, played in the mid '50's,
Hawkins, P	Pete	?	(Three-quarter), '61/2 season,
Hope,	Rowley	?	(Hooker?) original contacts led to the first Hilversum tour '58,

Player Name	known as	Dept/Office	Position, comments
Isaac, D J	Dave	POD ext 390	(Forward) Hilversum tour '60, V. Capt. 1st XV 62/3, later joined another travel company *Wakefield Fortune,* died suddenly in 1970's,
Jenkins, F	Fred	Uniformed Staff	Hilversum Tour '58, & visitors '59
Jenkins, I	Ivor	-	Fred's brother, Hilversum tour '58, played for the Royal Navy inter-services XV against the Army at Twickenham 1950's,
Keeling, D	Dave	FE - Notting Hill Gate	(Hooker), 'A' team Capt '64/5
Keston, D E	Don	POD ext 390	(Forward), founder member '53, ex Royal Navy, played for *Penarth,* Capt. Hilversum tour '58, Capt. 'A' team '59/61, left company to become a Bailiff, and played for *Wanstead RFC*
Knowles, R	Ralph	?	Played late 1950's
Lakin, M	Mike	CTD ext 376, later HTD, & WOR 4969	Played '60-65, 'A' team Capt '63/4, First team Capt '64/5,
Lidbetter, M A	Mike	Kensington High St. ext 672 & others	(Centre), Hilversum tours '58 & '60, 1st XV Capt '60/2 seasons,
Lowe, J	John	?	(Wing), 'A' team '60/1 season,
McCalla, M	Malcolm	London Office?	7-a-side runners up team '58
McCarthy, K	Keith	FE	(Wing forward), Hilversum tours '58 & '60,
MacKenzie, I	Ian	Press Office ext 530	(Forward); 'A' team vice Capt '62/3
McRitchie, C	Colin	?	(Wing forward), 'A' team Season '60/1,
Maidment, R L	Bob	FE MAN 2172 ext 16	(Scrum half), First team, Hilversum tour '60, 1st XV Capt '62/3, later joined a *Dutch S. African Bank,*

Player Name	known as	Dept/Office	Position, comments
Martin, H E	'Pincher' - Bert (Herbert, Eric)	Rates	(Hooker?) ex Royal Navy, played '59 Hilversum visitors, also cricket, pipe-smoker, died 2009, (Obit. TCPA *Bulletin'* issue 69) *'Pincher' is naval slang, for anyone named Martin, after 19th c. Admiral, a strict disciplinarian, putting ratings under arrest for any minor offence i.e. 'pinching them',*
Masterton-Smith, H	Harry	Harrods & others	(Forward-2nd row), First & 'A' team '60-62 transferred to Cook's Cairo office, in Spring '63
Mos, G A	Garry	? ext 587	(Forward), First team player '59/60, Hon. Treasurer '61-5,
Munnick, J	Jim	? LAN 4468 ext 2941	(Fly half), South African, 1st XV vice Capt '64/5,
New, J	Jack	-	(Forward), Hilversum tour '60, (tour only)
Petts, F	Freddie	POD	(Hooker), Hilversum tour '58,
Radley, A	Tony	Agents	(Wing Forward) left UK in late '60's to seek his fortune in Australia
Robertson, P	Pete	?	Season '60/1 'A' team
Rokosvinski, J	'Rocky' (Jurek)	?	(Centre) First and 'A' team player, '59-63, later believed to have joined *Swinton Rugby League Club,*
Samson, L	?	?	South African?, Season '60/1 'A' team
Sells, D	Derek	POD ext 226	(Forward -2nd row), Capt 'A' team '61/3, Vice Capt '64/5, Hilversum tour '58,
Shaw, P	Pete	Rates	(Centre), Hilversum tours "58 and '60,
Silk, B G	Gerry	CTD 2nd floor	(Scrum half), First and 'A' teams, '60/2 seasons, visited Harry Masterton-Smith in Cairo mid '60's
Simmons, P	Pete	Richmond & others	(Forward-2nd row), played mid '50's early '60's First & A team, also a London Society RU Referee,
Slader, T	Terry	?	Played early 1960's

Player Name	known as	Dept/Office	Position, comments
Smith, B	Brian	-	(Forward), Hilversum tour '60, (tour only)
Sutcliffe-Hey, S	Steve	?	(Full back), 'A' team player '61/2
Trenfield, W	Bill/Willie	CTD (Winter Sports)	Season '60/1 'A' team, later joined *Swiss Travel Service*,
Usher, J	John	HTD	(Wing Forward), Hilversum tour & 7-a-side team winners '58, visitors '59, later joined *Reuters*
Wade, M	Mark(cus)	-	(Hooker), Hilversum tour '60, worked for Irish airline *Aer Lingus*,
Wilson, G	Geoff	HTD	7-a-side Dept team winners '58
Wright, B	Brian	HTD	(Wing), Hilversum tour '60, 7-a-sides team '58, also played Hockey for company, keen darts player, later ran a travel agency in Sidmouth, Devon

Appendix 2: TCRFC fixture lists 1953 - 1965

Biggest recorded Wins and Losses - First and 'A' team

Wins	Date	Score	Losses	Date	Score
First XV			**First XV**		
LMS	1959	41-3	University College Hospital	1953	0-66
Old Masonians	1960	38-3	Westminster Bank	1965	0-46
HMS President	1960	33-0	London Scottish	1953	0-40
Brighton	1961	30-0	Meadhurst (BP)	1964	3-41
AEC	1960	30-3	Cuaco	1964	0-37
'A' XV			**'A' XV**		
Old Caterhamians	1961	56-0	AEC	1961	0-41
Barclays Bank	1960	29-0	Westminster Bank	1961	0-39
Cuaco	1963	25-0	Sidcup	1960	3-41
Woolwich Poly	1960	22-3	Hendon	1960	0-33
BBC	1962	23-5	Old Ignatians	1961	3-35

First post war revived season: 1953 – 54

Only fragments of fixture details have survived as follows:

Club XV Captain	R Dangerfield	Section Secretary	A Down ext 479

Date	Opponents	Venue	For	Against
1953				
31 Oct	London Scottish 'C'	?	0	40
7 Nov	Old Creightonians 'A'	?	0	21

14 Nov	University College Hospital	?	0	66
21 Nov	Southern Railway	?	16	3
28 Nov	Twickenham Exiles	?	0	12
5 Dec	Barclays Bank	?	9	17
12 Dec	Westminster Bank 'B'	?	6	9
19 Dec	Bank of England	?	0	6
1954				
Feb/Apr	No other details available	?		

Season	Opponents	Venue	F	A
1954 - 5	No details available			
1965 - 66	No details available			

Seven-a-sides competitions Business House (Eastern Banks) & North Kent

Year	Month	Results
1957	27 Apr - Gravesend	North Kent Sevens -No results recorded
1958	April - Inter-Departmental 7-a-side	Final HTD 8 – London Offices 6
1959	Apr 18, Sept 27	Eastern Banks -No results recorded
1961	September	Eastern Banks -No results recorded
1962	September	Eastern Banks -No results recorded

Easter Tour matches 1958 – 1965

1958	Opponents	Venue	F	A
Apr 5	Hilversum 'A'	Hilversum	33	0
Apr 6	Hilversum	Apeldoorn	3	3
1959				
Mar 28	Hilversum 'A'	Ravensbourne	No details available	
Mar 29	Hilversum	Ravensbourne		
1960				
Apr 16	t Gooi	Narden	14	6
Apr 17	Hilversum	Hilversum	13	9
1961				
Apr 1	Hilversum	Ravensbourne	No details available	
Apr 2	Hilversum 'A'	Ravensbourne		
1962				
Apr	Hilversum	Hilversum	No match	
1963				
Apr 13	Hilversum	Hilversum	No details available	
Apr 14	Delft / Leiden University?	Delft/Leiden		
1964				
Mar 28	Hilversum	Ravensbourne	0	0
Mar 29	Hilversum 'A'	Ravensbourne	0	3
1965				
Apr 17	Hilversum	Hilversum	No details available	
Apr 18	Delft / Leiden University?	Delft/Leiden		

Note: It is probable that the matches against the Dutch University students were either from Delft, *DSR-C –Delftsche Studenten Rugby Club*, or Leiden, *LSRG –Leisch Studenten Rugby Gezelschap*, as they had established clubs at the time – others were formed later.

Club XV Captain   R Dangerfield ?   Hon. Secretary   A Down ?

Opponents in (brackets) were original fixture before substitution

Date	Opponents	Venue	F	A
1955				
Sep 24	Westminster Bank 'B'	Away	5	6
Oct 1	Old Cestrians 'A'	Home	8	3
Oct 8	Saracens 'B'	Home	0	17
Oct 15	Old Mitchamians 'Ex. A'	Home	5	28
Oct 22	Sidcup Ex. B	Home	3	6
Oct 29	*(Old Dunstonians B)*			
	Osterley	Home	13	9
Nov 5	Chartered Bank of India	Away	6	25
Nov 12	Customs & Excise	Home	0	27
Nov 19	Woolwich Poly 'Ex. A'	Away	6	15
Nov 26	Ealing C	Home	6	6
Dec 3	Wasps C	Home	14	17
Dec 10	Southern Railway A	Home	19	3
Dec 17	GWR –Gt. Western Railways A	Away	9	3
Dec 31	Old Purleians 'Ex. A'	Home	8	10
1956				
Jan 7	Customs & Excise	Away	5	34
Jan 14	Chartered Bank of India	Home	0	6
Jan 28	Sidcup 'Ex. B'	Home	0	3
Feb 4	Old Caterhamians 'A'	Home	cancelled	
Feb 11	Southern Railway	Away	cancelled	
Feb 18	Lensbury 'Ex. A'	Home	cancelled	
Feb 25	Lyons A	Away	cancelled	
Mar 3	GWR -Great Western Railways A	Home	3	6
Mar 10	Old Anchorians 'Ex. A'	Home	15	0
Mar 17	Grasshoppers 'A'	Home	5	3
Mar 24	*(Foreign Office 1st)*			
	Rosslyn Park	Home	6	8
Mar 31	Old Tottonians 'Ex. A'	Away	cancelled	
Apr 7	Old Creightonians 'A'	Home	3	6
Apr 14	Civil Service 'B'	Home	6	0
Apr 21	Old Esthameians	Away	11	17

Fixtures	Canx	W	D	L	F	A
29	5	7	1	16	156	258

Season 1956 – 57

Club XV Captain   Don Keston   Vice Captain   Hugh Dalzell

Date	Opponents	Venue	F	A
1956				
22 Sep	Bank of London & S. America	?	30	0

Kicked into Touch

Sep/Dec	No records available			
1957				
Jan/Apr	No records available			
27 Apr	North Kent Sevens	Gravesend	?	?

Season 1957 – 58

Club XV Captain　　　Don Keston　　　　Vice Captain　　Hugh Dalzell

Date	Opponents	Venue	F	A
1957				
21 Sep	Saracens	Home	23	17
28 Sep	?			
5 Oct	Southern Railway	Home	0	25
12 Oct	?			
19 Oct	?			
26 Oct	London Hospital 'Ex B'	?	20	6
2 Nov	Lyons 'A'	Home	14	14
9 Nov	Old Anchorians	?	46	6
16 Nov	Sidcup 'Ex B'	?	11	12
23 Nov	Old Purlians	?	13	5
30 Nov	GWR 'A'	Ealing	0	8
7 Dec	Chartered Bank	Home	3	3
8 Dec	Old Shootershillians	Home	8	14
14 Dec	Old Caterhamians 'A'	Caterham	27	0
21 Dec	?			
28 Dec	Southern Railway 'A'	Raynes Park	6	3
1958				
Jan/Apr	No records available			

Season 1958– 59

Club XV Captain　　　H.A. Dalzell

Date	Opponents	Venue	F	A
1958/9				
Sep/Mar	No records available			
Mar 29	Hilversum (Holland)	Home		
Apr 4	Rochester 'A'	Home		
Apr 11	Merton & Morden	Home		
Apr 12	Cook's Inter-departmental 7-a-side competition	Home		
Apr 18	Silver Wing (BEA)	Northolt		
Apr 18	Eastern Banks Seven-a-side Ground of Std Bank of S. Africa)			

			(record up until March 29th)			
Fix.	P	W	D	L	F	A
28	24	13	2	9	323	146

Club Captain 1st.XV   H.A. Dalzell   Captain 'A' XV   D.E. Keston

Opponents in (brackets) were original fixture before substitution

D.	Opponents 1st' XV	V.	F	A	Opponents A' XV	V.	F	A
	Sept							
12	L.M.S Railway (practice match)	A	41	3	L.M.S Railway (practice match)	A		
19	London Scottish Ex. B	A	27	3				
26	Old Esthmeians A	H	17	6				
27	Business House 7 a sides	A						
	Oct							
3	A.E.C. A	A	20	3	Southern Railway Ex. C	H	6	19
10	Southern Railway A	A	9	0	Wimbledon A	A	5	6
11	Westminster Bank	H	3	5				
24	Ibis (Prudential)	A	0	32	London Scottish C	A	3	16
31	Old Olavians A	H	24	3	BBC A	A	14	0
	Nov							
7	Battersea Ironsides	H	3	6	Old Bec'hamians B	A	6	8
14	Juno	H	20	3	Old Cestrians Ex. A	A	6	11
21	Loughton Old Boys	A	11	19	Hermits	H	11	6
28	Hoover	A	12	0	Sun Alliance	H	11	38
	Dec							
5	Old Purleians	H	17	15	P.L.A. 'A' (Port Lon Auth)	A	19	8
6	No match				Swans Tours		cancelled	
12	Royal Free Hospital	A	3	6	(Royal Free. Hospital. A) HAC	A	18	13
19	Chartered Bank	H	8	12	(Foreign Office) Nat. Prov.Bk	A	3	6
	Jan							
2	Hoover	A	12	0	Sun Alliance	H	12	0
9	HMS President	H	33	0	Hendon	A	18	3

Kicked into Touch

D	Opponents 1st XV	V	F	A	Opponents A XV	V	F	A
17	U.S. Marines	H	cancelled		No match			
23	Cuaco (Com. Union)	H	11	9	Cuaco A (Com. Union)	A	3	22
30	BBC	A	11	26	Rochester Ex. A	H	13	8
Feb								
6	(Siemens A) Old Masonians	A	38	3	Old Caterhamians	H	3	10
13	Old Caterhamians	A (am)	cancelled		**England v Ireland Twickenham (8-5)**			
20	Old Isleworthians	A	6	10	Shirley Wanderers A	H	5	22
27	Standard Bank S. Africa	A	5	0	Old Purleians B	H	14	6
Mar								
5	Centymca A	H	20	3	Westcombe Park Ex. B	A	6	6
12	A.E.C. A	H	30	3	(Old Esthamians Ex. A) Battersea College	A	8	11
19	Ford A	A	9	19	Hermits	A	5	25
26	Sidcup Ex. B	A	19	8	Sidcup C	H	3	41
27	Forex (London Foreign Exc)	A						
Apr								
2	Lyons A	A	14	8	(Lyons B) Barclays Bank	H	29	0
9	Chartered Bank	A	cancelled		Woolwich Poly Ex. A	H	22	3
16	t Gooi (Holland)	A	14	6	Ruislip B	A	17	5
17	Hilversum (Holland)	A	13	9				

1st XV							A XV						
Fix.	C	W	D	L	F	A	Fix.	C	W	D	L	F	A
32	3	20	-	9	450	220	26	1	11	1	13	260	293

Season 1960 – 61

Club Capt 1st XV (Captaincy changed to)	Hugh Dalzell (M.A. Lidbetter)	Capt 'A' XV	D.E. Keston

D	Opponents 1st XV	V	F	A	Opponents A XV	V	F	A
Sep								
17	P.L.A. (Port Lon Authority)	A	3	26	No match			
24	Sudbury Court	H	9	19	Esher Ex. B	A	0	27

	Oct							
1	Sidcup Ex. A	H			Hendon B	A	0	33
8	Brighton A	H	0	6	Battersea College	A	3	0
15	Chartered Bank	A	8	11	Kings Coll. Hospital Ex. B	H	5	6
22	Decca	H	6	0	London Scottish Ex. C	A	11	12
29	London Fire Brigade	H	3	13	Old Cestrians B	A	0	17
	Nov							
5	Ibis (Prudential)	H	3	8	Decca A	A	Cancelled	
12	Southern Railway A	A	16	8	Southern Railway Ex. A	H	3	10
19	LMS Railway	A	Cancelled		LMS Railway A	H	20	0
26	Silver Wing (BEA)	A	8	6	Silver Wing (BEA)	H	6	0
	Dec							
3	Smiths (Clocks)	A	14	0	Ibis A (Prudential)	H	5	3
10	Juno	A	6	12	Esher Ex. B	H	9	12
17	Old Abbotstonians	H	15	0	Lloyds Bank B	A	0	3
24	Unilever	H	Cancelled		Unilever A	A	Cancelled	
31	Sun Alliance	A	5	10	Fairbairn House	H	0	0
	Jan							
7	Bank of West Africa	H	Cancelled					
8	Thos Cook 'A' XV	H	18	0	Thos Cook 1st XV	H	0	18
14	Custom & Excise	A	13	0	Old Colfeians Ex. B	H	3	9
21	Cuaco (Com. Union)	A			Cuaco A (Com. Union)	H	0	0
28	Toc H	A			Northern Poly B	H	0	3
	Feb							
4	Goldsmiths College	A			Battersea College 3rd	H	3	0
11	Kingston Tech. College	A			Kingston Tech. College A	H	Cancelled	
18	Battersea Ironsides	H			Sudbury Court A	A	3	9
	Mar							
4	Loughton O.B.	H			Old Elthamians C	A	22	3

11	Westminster Bank A	A				Westminster Bank C	H	0	39
19	U.S. Marines	H							
25	Chartered Bank	H				A.E.C. A	A	0	41
	Apr								
2	Hilversum (Holland)	H							
3						Hilversum 'A'	H		
8	Old Abbotstonians	A				Old Ignatians A	H	lost	
15	Old Caterhamians	H				Old Caterhamians B	A	56	0

Fix.	C	W	D	L	F	A	Fix	C	W	D	L	F	A
31	3	7	-	8	127	119	30	3	7	1	17	149	245

Season 1961 – 62

Club Captain 1st XV	M.A. Lidbetter	Captain 'A' XV	D. Sells
Vice-Captain 1st XV	H.A. Dalzell	Vice-Captain 'A' XV	G. Brooks

Opponents in (brackets) were original fixture before substitution

D	Opponents 1st XV	V	F	A	Opponents A XV	V	F	A
	Sep Business House 7-asides							
23	Trial match	H			Trial match	H		
30	V.C.D. (Vickers)	H	0	22	Ruislip B	A	0	40
	Oct							
7	Firestone	H	13	6	Old Ignatians A	A	3	35
14	Chartered Bank	A	5	0	Battersea College 3rd	H	17	3
21	Sun Alliance	H	6	11	Old Bec'hamians B	A	3	35
28	Ibis (Prudential)	A	3	10	Ibis A (Prudential)	H	8	3
	Nov							
4	London Scottish Ex. B	H	16	16	London Scottish Ex. C	A	16	0
11	Old Isleworthians	H	0	3				
18	London Irish Ex. A	H	5	9	Cuaco A (Com. Union)	A	8	37
25	Silver Wing (BEA)	H	0	16	Silver Wing (BEA) A	A	11	12
	Dec							
2	Cuaco (Com. Union)	H	3	3	HMS President	A	0	14

9	Southern Railway	A	0	14	Southern Railway A	H	8	5
16	London Fire Brigade	A	0	14	Nat. Prov. Bank Ex. B	A	12	3
23	Westminster Bank A	A	0	11				
30	Battersea Ironsides	H	Cancelled		Old Isleworthians A	A	Cancelled	

Jan

6	Standard Bank of South Africa	H	Cancelled		No match			
13	Sudbury Court	A	3	0	Sudbury Court A	H	3	11
27	A.E.C.	A	11	11	A.E.C. A	H	0	16

Feb

3	Firestone	A	18	0	Custom & Excise A	H	3	6
17	Decca	H	3	3	Decca A	A	17	3
24	Sidcup Ex. A	A	3	39	Sidcup C	H	0	25

Mar

3	*(Kingston TC)* Wanstead B	A	10	16	BBC A	A	23	5
10	*(Unilvever)* London French	*(A)* H	3	0	Unilever A	*A*	8	15
17	Harrodian	A	3	29	Battersea College 3rd	A	3	0
24	Ford Brigands	A	11	13	Ford Ex. A	H	0	6
31	Chartered Bank	H	3	3	Silver Wing (BEA) A	A	3	9

Apr

7	BBC	A	12	11	Hendon B	H	6	6
14	G.E.C.	H	0	0	Fairbairn House	A	Cancelled	
15	Thos Cook 'A' XV	H	17	0	Thos Cook 1st XV	H	0	17
	Hilversum	A	No match					

1st XV							**A XV**						
Fix	C	W	D	L	F	A	Fix	C	W	D	L	F	A
28	2	7	6	13	148	260	25	2	8	1	14	152	306

Club Captain 1st XV	R.L. Maidment			Captain 'A' XV	D. Sells		
Vice-Captain 1st XV	D.J. Isaac			Vice-Captain 'A' XV	I. MacKenzie		

Opponents in (brackets) were original fixture before substitution

D	Opponents '1st' XV	V	F	A	Opponents 'A' XV	V	F	A
	Sep Bus.House sevens							
22	Brighton A	A	30	0	No match			
29	Trial match	H			Trial match	H		
	Oct							
6	Battersea Ironsides	H	6	3	Battersea Ironsides A	A	12	13
13	Chartered Bank	H	6	3	Sudbury Court A	A	8	14
20	U.S. Marines	H	11	16	Northern Poly B	A	17	6
27	Firestone	H	Cancelled		Twickenham Ex. B	A	22	9
	Nov							
3	Old Hamptonians	H	0	20	Woolwich Poly Ex. A	A	19	11
10	V.C.D. (Vickers)	A	5	3	V.C.D. (Vickers) A	H	11	0
17	Ibis (Prudential)	H	0	11	Ibis A (Prudential)	A	16	12
24	Silver Wing (BEA)	A	3	0	Silver Wing (BEA) A	H	3	9
	Dec							
1	Southern Railway	H	3	15	Southern Railway A	A	0	22
8	Ford Brigands	H	5	5	Meadhurst A (BP)	A	Cancelled	
15	Customs & Excise	H	0	0	Customs & Excise A	A	8	11
22	Old Askeans B	H	Cancelled		Old Purleians Ex. B	A	Cancelled	
29	Firestone	A	Cancelled					
	Jan							
5	Chartered Bank	A	Cancelled		Battersea Ironsides	H	Cancelled	
12	Sun Alliance	A	Cancelled		Nat. Prov. Bank Bishops	H	Cancelled	
19	Old Caterhamians A	A	Cancelled		Battersea College 3rd	H	Cancelled	
26	L.M.S.	H	Cancelled		L.M.S. A	A	Cancelled	
	Feb							
2	Old Purleians B	A	Cancelled		Bank of West Africa	H	Cancelled	

9	Sudbury Court	H	Cancelled		Rams A	A	Cancelled	
16	Decca	A	Cancelled		Decca A	H	Cancelled	
	Mar							
2	London French	H	Cancelled		Toc H	A	15	0
9	C.A.V.	H	3	3	University Coll. Ex. B	A	Cancelled	
23	College of St. Mark & St. John	H	0	11	(C. St M & St J) Southall Tech.	A	10	16
30	Cuaco (Com. Union)	A	3	10	Cuaco A (Com. Union)	H	25	0
	Apr							
6	London Fire Brigade	H	0	3	Lyons B	A	15	13
13	Hilversum ?	A						
14	Hilversum	A						
20					Wanstead	A	3	15

!st XV							A XV						
Fix	C	W	D	L	F	A	Fix	C	W	D	L	F	A
26	11	5	3	7	75	103	24	9	8	-	8	184	151

Season 1963 – 64

Club Captain 1st XV	D J Isaac	Capt. 'A' XV	M Lakin
(taken over by)	(J Munnick)		
Vice-Captain 1st XV	R L Maidment	Vice-Captain 'A' XV	D Sells

Opponents in (brackets) were original fixture before substitution

D	Opponents '1st' XV	V	F	A	Opponents 'A' XV	V	F	A
	Sep							
21	Trial match	H			Trial match	H		
28	Battersea Ironsides	H	6	12	No match			
	Oct							
5	Ford Brigands	A	8	6	Battersea Ironsides 'A'	H	0	0
12	Chartered Bank	A	13	8	Old Elysians	H	3	9
19	Sudbury Court	A	0	18	Sudbury Court 'A'	H	3	9
26	Old Bec'hamians Extra 'A'	H	9	6	Royal Dental Hospital	A	5	8
	Nov							
2	Cuaco (Comm. Union)	H	0	23	Cuaco 'A' (Comm. Union)	A	3	6
9	Southern Railway	A	0	20	Southern Railway 'A'	H	0	18
16	U S Marines	H	Cancelled		C.A.V.	At	3	5
23	Kingston Tech. College	A	11	3	Battersea College 2nd	H	0	29

30	Ibis (Prudential)	A	0	8	(Ibis 'A') Chartered Bank	H	9	0
Dec								
7	Juno	H	8	0	Speedbird A (BOAC)	A	3	9
14	Old Caterhamians A'	H	6	3	Old Beccehamians 'B'	A	8	3
21	Customs & Excise	A	3	11	Customs & Excise 'A'	H	Cancelled	
28	Old Hamptonians	A	8	18	Wanstead			
Jan								
11	Sun Alliance	H	0	8	Nat Prov. Bank Bishops	A	Cancelled	
25	L.M.S.	A	17	9	(L.M.S 'A') Princes Gate ?	H	5	11
Feb								
1	V.C.D. (Vickers)	H	5	8	V.C.D. 'A'	A	3	3
15	London New Zealand	H	9	3	King Edward VII Nautical College	A	8	13
22	Royal Exchange Assurance	A	9	3	H.M.S. President	H	0	24
29	A.E.I. (Woolwich)	A	3	16	A.E.I. (Woolwich) 'A'	H	0	13
Mar								
7	Chartered Bank	H	11	3	Hendon 'B'	A	0	0
14	Plebs	H	3	8	Ford Extra 'A'	A	0	20
21	Decca	H	25	3	Decca 'A'	A	0	0
28	Hilversum (Holland)	H	0	0	Hilversum 'A'	H	0	3
Apr								
4	Silver Wings (BEA)	H	5	34	Silver Wing (BEA) 'A'	A	0	8
11	London Fire Brigade	A			London Transport 'A'	H		
18	Wanstead 'A'	H			Wanstead Extra 'A'	A		
25	Streatham 'A'				No match			

1st XV'							A XV						
Fix	C	W	D	L	F	A	Fix	C	W	D	L	F	A
28	1	11	1	12	159	231	26	2	2	2	17	53	191

Club Captain 1st XV		M. Lakin			Captain 'A' XV	D. Keeling		
Vice-Captain 1st XV		J. Munnick			Vice-Captain 'A' XV	D. Sells		

Opponents in (brackets) were original fixture before substitution

D	Opponents '1st' XV	V	F	A	Opponents 'A' XV	V	F	A
1964	**Sep**							
19	Trial match				Trial match	H		
26	London French	H	0	11	London French	A	Cancelled	
	Oct							
3	Battersea Ironsides	H	0	22	Saracens C	A		
10	Meadhurst (BP)	A	3	41	Meadhurst A (BP)	H		
17	Ibis (Prudential)	H			Ibis A (Prudential)	A		
24	Old Beccehamians Ex. A	H	3	6	Twickenham Ex. B	A		
31	Cuaco (Com Union)	A	0	37	Cuaco A	H		
	Nov							
7	Sudbury Court	H	6	16	Sudbury Court A	A		
14	Old Caterhamians A	A	0	21	Old Caterhamians B	H		
21	(Saracens B) Lyons	A	12	21	Lyons B	A		
28	Chartered Bank	A	3	34	Battersea Ironsides A	H		
	Dec							
5	Juno	A	0	9	Battersea College 3rd	A		
12	Twickenham Exiles	A	Cancelled		Old Beccehamians B	H		
19	Customs & Excise	H	14	31	Customs & Excise	A		
26	No match				No match			
1965	**Jan**							
2	Silver Wings (BEA)	A	8	22	Vetlab	H		
9	London New Zealand	H	6	16	No match			
16	Kingston Tech. College	A	3	5	Coll. of St. Mark & St. John	H		
23	G.E.C.	A	8	29	Nat. Prov. Bank Bishops	H		
30	Old Askeans B	A	0	16	Old Askeans C	H		
	Feb							
6	Westminster Bank A	H	0	46	Westminster Bank B	A		

13	Decca	A	6	11	Decca A	H		
20	Southern Railway	H			Southern Railway A	A		
Mar								
6	Coll. of St. Marks & St. John	H			Borough Polytechnic	A		
13	Chartered Bank	H			Ford Ex. A	A		
27	C.A.V.	A			C.A.V. 'A'	H		
Apr								
3	London Fire Brigade	H			Silver Wings (BEA) A	A		
10	Lyons A	H			Wanstead Ex. B	A		
17	Hilversum (Holland)	A			Hilversum (Holland)	A		

1st XV							A XV					
Fix	C	W	D	L	F	A	Fix	W	D	L	F	A
26	1	0	-	18	72	294	26					

Appendix 3: TCRFC - opponents, in most frequent fixture order 1953-1965
Based on surviving fixture lists for First and 'A' XV teams

Club	Fix	Club	Fix
Southern Railway *(now Raynes Park RFC)*	17	London Fire Brigade	4
Chartered Bank of India *(now Standard Chartered Bank)*	16	London French	4
Cuaco *(Commercial Union Assurance Co.- now Aviva)*	12	Saracens	4
Silver Wings *BEA (now British Airways)*	11	Twickenham Exiles	4
Battersea Ironsides	10	U.S. Marines	4
Custom & Excise *(now Customs Corsairs)*	10	College of St. Mark & St. John *(now Univ. Coll. Plymouth -Marjon)*	3
Decca *(now Teddington RFC)*	10	G.W.R *(Great Western Railways)*	3
Ibis *(Prudential)*	10	Meadhurst BP (Sunbury, Middx)	3
Old Caterhamians	10	Old Askeans	3
Sudbury Court *(now Sudbury & London Springboks –merging with Hayes RFC)*	10	Old Cestrians	3
Battersea College *(now University of Surrey)*	8	Old Esthameians	3
Lyons *(now Centaurs RFC)*	8	Old Isleworthians	3

Sidcup	8	Unilever	3
Westminster Bank (now NatWest)	8	Woolwich Poly (now University of Greenwich)	3
L.M.S (London Midland Scottish Railway)	7	AEI (Woolwich)	2
London Scottish	6	Barclays Bank	2
Old Beccehamians (now Beccehamians)	6	Brighton (now Brighton Blues)	2
Old Purleians	6	Esher	2
Sun Alliance (now Holbrook RFC)	6	G.E.C. (General Electric Company)	2
Wanstead	6	Hermits (now Bexley RFC)	2
A.E.C. (Assoc. Equipment Co.- merged with GWR)	5	HMS President (London Div. RNR)	2
Ford	5	Hoover	2
Kingston Technical College (now Kingston University)	5	London New Zealand	2
National Provincial Bank (now NatWest)	5	Loughton Old Boys	2
V.C.D. (Vickers, Crayford)	5	Northern Poly (now Lon.Metropolitan University)	2
BBC	4	Old Abbotstonians	2
C.A.V. (Acton, Middx)	4	Old Anchorians (now Gillingham Anchorians RFC)	2
Firestone (Gunnersbury)	4	Old Creightonians	2
Hendon	4	Old Hamptonians	2
Juno (Kent)	4	Old Ignatians (now Enfield-Ignatians RFC)	2
P.L.A. -Port of London Authority (now Ravens RFC)	2	Old Shootershillians (now Shooters Hill RFC)	1
Royal Free Hospital (merged with University & Middx)	2	Plebs	1
Ruislip	2	Princes Gate ?	1
Standard Bank of South Africa (now Standard Chartered Bank)	2	Rochester (now Medway RFC)	1
Bank of England	1	Rosslyn Park	1
Bank of London & South America (now Lloyds TSB)	1	Royal Dental Hospital (now Barts & RDH)	1
Borough Polytechnic (now London South Bank University)	1	Royal Exchange Assurance (merged with Guardian Assurance –now AXA)	1
Centymca	1	Shirley Wanderers	1
Civil Service	1	Smiths (Clocks)	1

Ealing	1	Old Mitchamians	1
(now Ealing Trailfinders RFC)			
Fairbairn House (Boys Club)	1	Old Olavians	1
Forex	1	Osterley	1
(London Foreign Exchange)			
Goldsmiths College	1	Old Colfeians	1
(part of University of London)			
Grasshoppers (Middx)	1	Old Elthamians	1
HAC *(Honourable Artillery Company)*	1	Old Elysians	1
Harrodian *(now Barnes RFC)*	1	Old Masonians *(now Teddington RFC)*	1
King's College Hospital	1	Southall Technical College	1
King Edward VII Nautical College *(now Lon. Metropolitan University)*	1	Speedbird (BOAC) *(now British Airways)*	1
London Irish	1	Streatham *(now Streatham & Croydon RFC)*	1
London Hospital *(now Royal Hospitals RFC)*	1	University Coll. Hospital *(merged with Royal Free & Middx)*	1
London Transport	1	Vetlab *(Gov. Central Veterinary Lab.)*	1
Merton & Morden *(now just Merton)*	1		

Ravensbourne Kent, unknown match and date –probably 1950's
Where's the ball –kicked into touch? – says it all really!

During research for this book I frequently came across references to the amateur game not being what it once was, and that professionalism has ruined the game and so on.

As I was near completing the writing, my wife and I visited our daughter in Derbyshire for a birthday celebration –held coincidentally in their local rugby clubhouse. The following day a Sunday, I accompanied my son in law and two grandsons' to attend an away match for their club. As they are eight and six respectively – they play mini and tag rugby. This is how they are shown the basics of the game in a fun way –with the inevitable support of many parents and volunteers. It was thrilling to watch their determination and sheer enjoyment running with the ball –with enthusiastic coaches shouting instructions. It all helped create a carnival atmosphere on a cold –but sunny autumn morning.

What struck me then, was in a sense nothing has changed in forty years. Whilst of course the training, equipment and facilities are all much better –the grass roots basics and amateur enthusiasm are still there. I know because I found myself shouting encouragement too –albeit from the comfort of the touch line whilst enjoying a welcome bacon butty and hot coffee.

Author - John Dann spent forty years in the travel industry in a wide range of disciplines from retail & business sales, marketing, advertising, and tour operation. Beginning with Thomas Cook, later the Thomson Organisation, P&O and American Express. During his career he managed the travel arrangements of prominent business houses such as Rolls Royce and Times Newspapers and celebrities including actor Peter Sellers, and author Alistair Mclean. He is widely travelled, has written and designed travel brochures and contributed many trade press articles. He returned to Thomas Cook when it operated a worldwide conference and incentive management business in London. As marketing manager he re-branded the Cook's Travel Bonds into the Worldwide Travel Vouchers and authored 'Travel Incentives', a booklet promoting their benefits. It was distributed to Cook's business clients throughout their worldwide office network in the early 1990's. Spends his time walking his Labrador on the Sussex Downs and watching rugby, subsidises his passion for travel and sailing by writing articles.

Johndann@ntlworld.com

Photo taken after a good lunch
prior to the England v Ireland game
at Twickenham February 2010